If Kallimos had a chef . . .

it would be Debra Stark.

On the mythical island of Kallimos (as you will read) natural foods are a way of life. In West Concord, Massachusetts, Debra's Natural Gourmet food store is a way of life, too. Rated one of the top natural food stores in the country, it was founded by Debra Stark in 1989. In addition, Debra is the founder and president of Stark Sisters, Inc., a company that manufactures award-winning, gourmet granolas praised by the likes of *Bon Appétit, The Boston Globe,* and the *Chicago Tribune.*

Often asked to speak about food and its connection to health, Debra is frequently consulted by television shows and doctors who call her for natural and complementary alternatives to standard drug therapy. She writes columns on health and nutrition for newspapers, consumer periodicals, and other publications.

Though she wasn't raised on Kallimos, Debra has eaten naturally since the day she was born. Everything about Debra's life is in harmony with the principles of Kallimos. Indeed, it's as though she were destined to become its chef.

If Kallimos Had a Chef

NATURAL RECIPES

FOR A

NATURAL WORLD

Debra Stark

VanderWyk & Burnham
Acton, Massachusetts

Published by VanderWyk & Burnham
A Division of Publicom, Inc.
P.O. Box 2789, Acton, Massachusetts 01720

Excerpts are from *Learning from Hannah: Secrets for a Life Worth Living* by William H. Thomas, M.D. © 1999, published by VanderWyk & Burnham, Acton, Mass. The excerpts are included by arrangement with the author. Recipes originally appeared in *Round-the-World Cooking at the Natural Gourmet*, by Debra Stark.

Both *If Kallimos Had a Chef* and *Learning from Hannah* are available for quantity purchases. For information on bulk discounts, call (800) 789-7916 or write to Special Sales at the above address.

Library of Congress Cataloging-in-Publication Data
Stark, Debra.
    If Kallimos had a chef : natural recipes for a natural world/Debra Stark.
        p. cm.
    Consists of recipes which originally appeared in the book entitled: Round-the-world cooking at the Natural Gourmet and excerpts from the fictional account: Learning from Hannah.
    Includes index.
    ISBN 1-889242-15-2
    1. Cookery (Natural foods) I. Stark, Debra. Round-the-world cooking at the Natural Gourmet. II. Thomas, William H., M.D. Learning from Hannah. III. Title.

TX741 .S734 2001
641.5'63—dc21   2001026161

Interior book design by Joan Dakai, Publicom, Inc.

Visit our Web site at www.vandb.com

FIRST PRINTING
Manufactured in the United States of America
10 9 8 7 6 5 4 3 2 1

Why Kallimos?

Kallimos is an imaginary island where life is simple and kind. Kallimos grew from the life experiences of William H. Thomas, M.D., who shares his vision of a better world in an adventure tale called *Learning from Hannah: Secrets for a Life Worth Living.* Dr. Thomas portrays a society where the wisdom of elders creates goodness, and a land where the comforting cycles of nature are revered.

I keep trying to remember what I felt the first time I read *Learning from Hannah.* I remember I was profoundly moved and determined to behave, think, and feel differently toward the world around me. I remember feeling grateful, too, to my parents because they encouraged me to appreciate individuality and to respect that which I may not understand.

The people on the island of Kallimos live simply and naturally, something I've tried to do all my life—especially with regard to food. While other kids took Twinkies to school, I brought fresh pineapple or dates stuffed with peanut butter. My mother served us organic oranges she picked alongside our friend Mr. Ogeltree. She made whole grain bread with nuts and seeds. My mother would have been right at home on Kallimos.

Characters in *Learning from Hannah* use stories to teach the lessons of Kallimos. In particular, I loved the stories about community, about growing, preparing and sharing food because I believe natural foods are part of a simpler life and a simpler time. Natural foods nourish body and soul, and the small moments when one shares a simple meal with family or friends are as important as the birth of a child or the death of a loved one.

Excerpts from *Learning from Hannah* appear as part of the section openers in this cookbook. They will give you a glimpse of Kallimos. The people you'll meet include Bill and Jude, a couple shipwrecked on the island; Hannah, their teacher; Haleigh, the village gardener and Hannah's teacher as well; and Zachary, one of the children on the island.

Now go and find joy and comfort in these recipes.

Debra Stark
Summer 2001

Contents

If Kallimos Had a Chef

Cooking the Natural Way

What are natural foods? Natural foods are foods that have not been overrefined or treated with chemicals and that do not contain harmful additives.

A whole-food diet is not necessarily vegetarian—all the food groups are represented. For this reason, poultry and fish are included.

Not all recipes in this book are meant to be eaten regularly. Some desserts are high in fat content, but when you want to splurge, they are heavenly. Luscious and decadent can be natural, too!

FUNDAMENTALS

All vegetables and fruits—organic whenever possible—are washed before use.

Apart from onions and garlic, vegetables are not peeled unless specified. Vitamins and minerals lie just beneath the surface.

Save liquid from steaming vegetables and cooking beans to use in soups, stew, etc. Stock is rich in nutrients and adds flavor.

Eggs are large and free-range. In spite of the bad press, eggs are a wonderful food. They contain both unsaturated and saturated fats, and are rich in lecithin, the cholesterol emulsifier, as well as choline, pyridoxine, and inositol. They are also rich in vitamin A and are an excellent protein source.

Salt in this book always means sea salt, made from evaporated seawater. It is rich in minerals.

Baking powder should always be aluminum free. There are several brands available.

LEGUMES (peas and beans)

Legumes or dried beans may well be the nutritional stars of the plant world. Low in fat and high in the kind of fiber that lowers cholesterol, they also contain components that are protective against cancer. When combined with grains, nuts, or seeds, they are an excellent protein source. Legumes, stored away from sunlight and moisture, last for years. Beans excavated from Incan temples were capable of germination!

Always sort and rinse legumes before use to check for stones and debris. Refer to the chart that follows for cooking times. Once cooked and cooled, legumes may be kept for several days in the refrigerator, or they may be frozen. To freeze, cool and pack into jars, leaving 1/2 inch at the top for expansion.

The amount of water used for cooking legumes is generally 3 to 4 times their volume, or to a level of 2 inches above the beans, with more boiling water added as necessary during cooking.

LEGUMES (Dried Beans, Peas, and Lentils)	SOAKING TIME	REGULAR COOKING TIME	PRESSURE COOKING TIME
Adzuki beans	3–4 hours	1 hour	15 minutes
Black-eyed peas	8–12 hours	1-1/2 hours	10–15 minutes
Black turtle beans	3–4 hours	1 hour	10–15 minutes
Cannellini beans	8–12 hours	1-1/2 hours	20 minutes
Chickpeas	8–12 hours	3 hours	25 minutes
Kidney beans	8–12 hours	1-1/2–2 hours	20 minutes
Lentils, brown	none	20 minutes	
Lentils, red	none	15 minutes	
Lima beans	4–8 hours	1-1/2 hours	20 minutes
Mung beans	4–8 hours	45 minutes	10 minutes
Navy beans	8–12 hours	1-1/2 hours	20 minutes
Pinto beans	8–12 hours	1-1/2 hours	20 minutes
Soybeans	8–12 hours	3 hours	50 minutes
Split peas, green	none	1–1-1/2 hours	
Split peas, yellow	none	1-1/2 hours	

Though it is traditional to soak beans, one can skip that step by simply bringing beans to a boil uncovered, and boiling vigorously for 10 minutes to release the gases. Then, cover and simmer until soft. Don't soak beans when using a pressure cooker.

Do not add salt or acidic ingredients, such as tomatoes, until legumes are almost finished cooking. Adding during cooking toughens legumes.

Substitute canned beans in any recipe. Drain and rinse first.

Usually 1 pound dry beans = 2 cups dry = 5–6 cups cooked.

GRAINS

Except for bulgur and couscous, grains are cooked by bringing the correct amount of cooking liquid to a boil in a pot large enough to accommodate the increase in volume after cooking. (Don't forget to use up that vegetable stock!) Add grain to boiling liquid, stir once, allow liquid to return to boiling, turn heat down low, cover pot, and cook grains until they are soft. Do not stir grains after they come to a boil because too much stirring makes them gummy.

GRAIN	BOILING WATER to GRAIN	COOKING TIME
Amaranth	3 to 1	20–25 minutes
Barley, hulled	3 to 1	60–90 minutes
Barley, pearled	2 to 1	45 minutes
Buckwheat	2 to 1	15–20 minutes
Bulgur	1 to 1	pour boiling water over
Cornmeal	3 to 1	20–25 minutes
Couscous	1 to 1	pour boiling water over
Millet	2-1/2 to 1	25–30 minutes
Oats, rolled	2 to 1	20–30 minutes
Oats, steel cut	3 to 1	30 minutes
Quinoa	2 to 1	10 minutes
Rice, brown	2 to 1	45 minutes
Rice, wild	2 to 1	45–60 minutes

For hard grains, such as wheat, rye, and barley, it is also possible to place them in a pot together with the water and bring them to a boil at the same time. Cook as above. Using this method for cooking rice makes it creamier.

Add salt to grains at the end because it slows the cooking process.

For bulgur and couscous, simply pour boiling water over the grain and stir once. Let grain sit for about 15–20 minutes until all the water is absorbed.

For fluffier grains, stir with a fork after grain is cooked and let sit, covered, in pot for an additional 10 minutes.

Should your rice be sticky, stir in several spoonfuls of soy granules. Allow pot to stand covered for 10 minutes. Not only will the granules absorb excess moisture, but they will give the rice a nutty flavor and a gourmet look.

Store grains in a cool, dry place. The freezer is perfect! Heat and moisture are the main causes of deterioration.

GRATING

Pecorino Romano cheese is a flavorful sheep's milk cheese tolerated well by many people who can't have dairy products. To grate it, place Romano that has been cut into 1- to 2-inch cubes into the work bowl of a food processor. Using the steel blade, grate about 2 cups at a time. Turn machine on and off several times and then let it run until the cheese is grated. Grate more than you need for a particular recipe so that you have extra on hand. Store it in the refrigerator or freezer.

GREASING

Use a film of 1/2 soya lecithin and 1/2 vegetable oil or butter. Liquid lecithin alone is too thick to spread easily. Diluting it with oil works like a charm. Always keep a jar of the lecithin-oil mixture on hand to grease with.

To grease, use a pastry brush to spread the mixture. Natural grains tend to stick to pans but will not when you use lecithin to grease.

SWEETENERS

No sweetener can be eaten with impunity and their use is often debated. The recipes use primarily honey or maple syrup for sweetening. Other options are fruit juice concentrates, rice syrup, barley malt, date sugar (made from dried pulverized dates), Sucanet, Rapurada, and the South American herb Stevia.

Honey is also a healer. Germs won't grow in honey, and when applied to a cut or burn, it works magic. Should your honey crystallize, set the jar in a bowl of hot water until the crystals have dissolved.

TAHINI AND SESAME BUTTER

Sesame paste (tahini) is made from hulled toasted sesame seeds. Sesame butter uses unhulled sesame seeds. Use interchangeably. Both are wonderful sources of protein, but sesame butter has far more calcium.

TAMARI and SHOYU

Soy sauces are fermented soybean liquids that rise to the top when miso is made. Tamari and shoyu, unlike other soy sauces, are processed without chemicals and are rich in flavor. Tamari is wheat free, while shoyu is not.

BREADS

A teaspoon of sweetener activates yeast. Yeast should become foamy after 10 minutes when mixed with lukewarm water and a natural sugar. If not, start over. Either the water temperature is too hot or cold, or your yeast is bad.

Store dry baking yeast in the freezer in an air-tight container, where it will keep forever.

To rise, dough must be warm and kept in a draft-free location. Plastic wrap or a shower cap keeps the dough warm and keeps out drafts. When you cover the dough with a towel, be careful not to place where there is a draft.

Save soured milk for use in muffins. Nothing makes them rise better. There will be no hint of sourness in the final product.

Measuring Simplified

1 teaspoon	=	1/3 tablespoon
1 tablespoon	=	3 teaspoons
2 tablespoons	=	1 fluid ounce
4 tablespoons	=	1/4 cup
5-1/3 tablespoons	=	1/3 cup or 2-2/3 ounces
8 tablespoons	=	1/2 cup
16 tablespoons	=	1 cup
1 cup	=	1/2 pint or 8 fluid ounces
2 cups	=	1 pint or 16 fluid ounces
1 pint liquid	=	16 fluid ounces or 2 cups
1 quart liquid	=	2 pints or 4 cups
1 gallon	=	4 quarts
16 dry ounces	=	1 pound
1 stick butter	=	8 tablespoons
4 cups flour	=	1 pound
8 ounce can	=	1 cup
one ounce	=	6 teaspoons, 2 tablespoons, 1/8 cup
2 cups liquid	=	1 pound
1/2 whole egg	=	about 2 tablespoons
5 whole eggs	=	1 cup
8–9 whites	=	1 cup
12 yolks	=	1 cup

1/2 pint cream	=	1 cup or 2 cups whipped		
6 1/2-inch slices dry bread	=	1 cup bread crumbs		
1 pound nutmeats	=	4-1/2 cups, about 3-1/2 cups chopped		
1 pound dry beans	=	2 cups dry	=	5–6 cups cooked

Breakfasts

Back at Kallimos . . .

We awoke again in the dark when a woman entered our quarters. She sat us up in bed and helped us each drink a cup of bitter tea. I remember little of what she said, but she spoke to us in English and her voice carried the delicate trace of a southern accent. Before she left, she promised to return in the morning.

We slept soundly, without dreaming, and awoke at dawn. At first we lay in bed, whispering our thoughts to each other, but as the minutes passed and the daylight gathered strength, we managed to sit up and examine our surroundings.

Standing like attendants around our bed were four large rose-colored urns. About three feet high, they tapered gently from the mouth to the base. A riot of flowers and herbs issued forth from each, filling the room with the subtle yet distinctive aroma of life and growth.

The urns stood on a floor that was a spectacular mosaic of tiny, brightly colored tiles. The tiles formed swirls that curled around and flowed through each other. If a dozen sunsets had been mixed together and brought indoors, it could not have been more beautiful.

continued . . .

. . . Two east-facing windows filled the room with light. In the center were four low wooden benches, each about a foot high and two feet long. They surrounded a small fire pit made of dry laid stone. . . . Looking up, we saw a smoke hole in the ceiling above the fire pit. Clay pots filled with deep red, magnificently petaled flowers hung from the ceiling above our bed.

Jude whispered, "It's like being inside and outside at the same time."

Excerpted from Learning from Hannah © *William H. Thomas, M.D.*

APPLE TOAST

Serves 4

Equally delicious with fresh peaches or apricots. Try mashing fresh berries to mix with honey and cinnamon.

**8 apples, peeled, cored and
   quartered
1/3 cup honey
1/2 teaspoon cinnamon**

**8 slices whole wheat bread
8 teaspoons butter**

Coarsely chop apples using the steel blade of a food processor. Place chopped apples in a pot together with honey and cinnamon. Cook for 5 minutes over medium high heat, until apples are fragrant and tender.

Toast the bread and place two slices per person on warm plates. Butter each slice with a teaspoon of butter and top with warm apple mixture.

Serve immediately with a glass of milk or cup of herbal tea.

BLUEBERRY BUTTERMILK PANCAKES

Makes 6

For blueberry lovers! Best with wild blueberries. Great even with frozen, unsweetened berries.

1/2 cup whole wheat pastry flour	**1 teaspoon vanilla**
1 tablespoon toasted wheat germ	**1/4 teaspoon cinnamon**
1 tablespoon soy flour	**1 teaspoon baking powder**
3 eggs	☐
1/2 cup sour or buttermilk, or soy milk	**1/2 cup blueberries**

Blend ingredients, except for blueberries, using a wire whisk, or the steel blade of a food processor and on/off turns. If using the processor, stop the machine once or twice to scrape down the sides of the workbowl with a rubber spatula.

Ladle pancake batter by 1/4 cupfuls onto hot, buttered griddle. Bake until bubbles form and begin to pop on the unbaked side. Press blueberries into the surface of pancakes and flip.

Bake pancakes until brown on the second side. Serve at once with maple syrup or honey.

CORNMEAL MOLASSES WAFFLES

Makes 12

Dark because of molasses, but light and crunchy due to cornmeal.

2 eggs
1 cup sour or buttermilk
1/4 cup safflower or canola oil
1/4 cup Barbados molasses

1 cup cornmeal
1/3 cup whole wheat pastry flour
1/2 teaspoon salt
2 teaspoons baking powder

Preheat and oil waffle iron using a pastry brush and a mixture of oil and liquid lecithin.

Blend all ingredients using a wire whisk or an electric blender.

Use 1/2 cup batter per waffle. Cook waffles until the light on the waffle iron goes out, signifying waffles are cooked. Serve at once with maple syrup or honey.

DATE CORIANDER WAFFLES

Makes 12

Pour melted butter mixed with maple syrup or honey over date coriander waffles and watch them go!

1 cup sweet, sour, or soy milk
2 eggs
1 cup whole wheat pastry flour
1/4 cup bran
1 teaspoon baking powder
1/4 teaspoon coriander

1/2 cup date sugar (or date
    pieces rolled in oat flour)
□
1/3 cup melted butter
1/3 cup maple syrup or honey

Preheat waffle iron; brush the grids with a mixture of liquid lecithin and oil or melted butter.

Combine the ingredients (except melted butter and syrup or honey) using the steel blade of a food processor and 10 quick on/off turns.

Bake waffles using 1/3 cup batter per waffle until the signal light on the waffle iron goes out, signifying waffles are ready to take out.

In the meantime, melt butter together with maple syrup.

Serve waffles with topping mixture drizzled on top.

DEB'S GRANOLA

Makes 12 servings

For almond lovers - the best granola ever! Allergies? Feel free to substitute grains.

1/2 cup unsweetened coconut	1/4 cups wheat bran
3 cups sliced almonds	☐
2 cups rolled oats	1 cup maple syrup
1 cup wheat flakes	1/4 cup canola or safflower oil
1 cup rye flakes	1 teaspoon vanilla extract
1 cup barley flakes	1/4 teaspoon salt, optional

Preheat oven to 300 degrees.

Mix dry ingredients in a large bowl. (If you don't have a large enough bowl, divide dry ingredients between two, for example, 1 cup rolled oats in one bowl, and 1 cup oats in a second.) Pour wet ingredients over dry and mix well using your hands or a rubber spatula. Make sure all the grains are well-coated.

Spread granola in shallow pans and bake in the oven until golden brown and dry, about 1-1/2 hours. Stir every 15-20 minutes. Baking time varies due to weather, the size of your pans, your oven, etc.

When granola is dry and golden brown, remove from oven and stir. Let cool completely before storing in airtight containers.

MEXICAN CHILE WAFFLES

Makes 12

A spicy, filling way to start the day. Serve Mexican Chile Waffles as a weekend lunch or dinner.

- **1 pound cheddar cheese, or 1 pound soy cheese**
- **1-1/3 cups sweet, sour, or soy milk**
- **2 plum tomatoes**
- **4 eggs**
- **1 cup yellow cornmeal**
- **2/3 cup whole wheat pastry flour**
- **1 tablespoon baking powder**
- **1 teaspoon chili powder**
- **1/4 cup favorite salsa, medium or hot**

Preheat waffle iron; brush grids with a mixture of liquid lecithin and melted butter or oil.

Grate cheddar cheese with the shredding disk of food processor using firm pressure. Remove grated cheese from work bowl.

Combine remaining ingredients using the steel blade and 10 quick on/off turns. Add cheese and mix in with 2 on/off turns.

Bake waffles using 1/3 cup batter per waffle until signal light on the waffle iron goes out, signifying waffles are ready to remove.

Serve immediately with extra salsa.

A good pepperjack cheese can be used if you like your food extra sharp and spicy!

MOLASSES-MAPLE-NUTTY GRANOLA

Makes 12 servings

Dark and rich, high in iron.

1 cup maple syrup	**6 cups oats**
1/2 cup blackstrap molasses	**1 cup walnut halves**
1/4 cup canola oil	**2 cups pecan halves**
☐	**2 cups pumpkin seeds**
4 teaspoons cinnamon	**1/2 cup sunflower seeds**

Preheat oven to 300 degrees.

Combine wet ingredients. Combine dry ingredients. (If you don't have a bowl large enough, divide ingredients between two bowls, for example, 3 cups oats in one bowl, and 3 cups oats in the second.) Pour wet ingredients over dry and mix well using your hands or a rubber spatula.

Divide granola between shallow baking pans and bake in a 300 degree oven until roasted and dry, about 1-1/2 hours. Stir every 15-20 minutes.

Let granola cool completely before storing in air-tight containers.

POPPY SEED CARDAMOM WAFFLES

Makes 12

Poppy seeds are a real treat. Cardamom, used in holiday baking, makes a special appearance and adds a heavenly fragrance.

1-1/3 cups sweet, sour, or soy milk	1-1/2 teaspoons baking powder
2 eggs	1/2 teaspoon salt
1/4 cup melted butter, safflower or canola oil	1/4 teaspoon cardamom
1/4 cup honey	1 tablespoon orange rind
1-1/4 cups whole wheat pastry flour	2 tablespoons poppy seeds

Preheat waffle iron; brush the grids with a mixture of liquid lecithin and oil or melted butter.

Blend all ingredients, except the poppy seeds, using the steel blade of a food processor and 10 quick on/off turns. Orange rind will be "grated." Add poppy seeds and scrape down the sides of the workbowl with a rubber spatula. Turn the food processor on and off quickly once or twice.

Bake waffles using 1/3 cup batter per waffle until signal light on waffle iron goes out, signifying waffles are ready to take out.

Top with honey or maple syrup and serve immediately.

PUMPKIN CORNCAKES

Makes 12

Leftover cooked sweet potatoes or squash can be substituted for pumpkin with equally delicious results.

1/2 cup cornmeal	1 tablespoon honey
1/2 cup cooked pumpkin	1 cup boiling water
1 cup whole wheat flour	1 cup sweet, sour, or soy milk
1/2 teaspoon salt	2 teaspoons baking powder
1 egg	

Blend all the ingredients using the steel blade of a food processor or an electric blender until the batter is smooth.

Ladle batter by 1/4 cupfuls onto hot, buttered griddle. Bake until bubbles form and begin to pop on the uncooked surface. Flip and brown on second side.

Serve hot with honey or maple syrup.

SHASHOUKA

Serves 4

Of Greek origin, great for Sunday brunch.

1/4 cup olive oil
6 potatoes scrubbed, unpeeled
   and diced
1 red bell pepper, thinly sliced
1 green bell pepper, thinly sliced
2 onions, finely chopped
   ☐
2/3 cup tomato sauce

1 small dried chile pepper
1/2 teaspoon dried basil
1/2 teaspoon dried oregano
1/2 teaspoon salt
1/2 teaspoon black pepper
   ☐
8 eggs

In a large skillet, gently warm olive oil. Add potatoes, bell peppers and onions. Stir for 3 minutes. Add tomato sauce, herbs and spices, and cook another 3 minutes.

Reduce heat to low. Cover skillet and cook vegetables until tender, about 30 minutes. Stir several times during cooking to prevent sticking.

(Shashouka can be prepared up to this point one day in advance. Cool completely, cover, refrigerate. Reheat before continuing.)

Increase heat to medium-low. Break eggs on top of potato mixture. Cover and simmer about 3-4 minutes, or until eggs are set. Serve immediately.

Appetizers

Back at Kallimos . . .

It was the aroma of food being cooked over an open fire that drove us from our bed. Getting up was painful. Our muscles and joints were not only bruised but stiff with disuse as well. Together, we leaned forward and, using each other for support, brought ourselves to a standing position. We held each other tight and thanked God that we were alive.

The sound of the front door opening pulled us apart. The woman from the night came into the room. This time, she brought a tray loaded with dishes of steaming food and two teapots.

In English, she invited us to sit down on the benches in the center of the room. With little prompting from our visitor, we began to eat. We shoveled down mouthful after mouthful of the delicious offerings, and when our plates were empty, she refilled them. As we ate, she told us the story of our arrival in this country.

"For three days before you came here, a great storm held us in its grasp. It came from

continued . . .

the west, and not even the oldest soul among us can remember a storm with such great power. All of the trees bowed before the wind, and the rain came down like a river from the sky. We were frightened and did not dare stir from our homes. You can imagine our joy when the storm passed over the mountains. . . .

. . . "Zachary, one of the boys from our village, was the first down to the shore after the storm broke. I'm afraid you gave him quite a scare when he came upon you. He thought you were dead. He ran back to the village, calling to us in full voice. We carried you here and laid you down in this bed. Few believed that you would survive the night. It is your good fortune that they were wrong."

Excerpted from Learning from Hannah © *William H. Thomas, M.D.*

BABAGANOUSH

Makes about 4 cups

Loved throughout the Middle East, babaganoush is served with pita or vegetables, garnished with spicy black olives and a little paprika sprinkled on top.

2 large eggplants	**1/4 teaspoon cumin**
□	**2/3 cup sesame tahini**
4 cloves garlic	**1/4 cup lemon juice**
1/2 teaspoon salt	**pinch cayenne pepper**
	paprika to garnish

Prick eggplants with knife so they won't explode in the oven. Bake on a cookie sheet until the eggplant meat feels soft. Cool slightly and then scrape eggplant out of skin and place in the workbowl of a food processor. (Instead of baking eggplants, they may also be steamed in a pot with water until soft.)

Using the steel blade of a food processor, blend eggplant meat with garlic, salt, cumin, tahini and lemon juice until desired smoothness has been achieved.

Spoon babaganoush into a bowl and serve at room temperature. Store in the refrigerator for up to 2 weeks. If desired, freeze.

BLACK BEAN DIP

Makes about 8 cups

Similar to guacamole, without fat, black bean dip is a real crowd pleaser! Serve it with your favorite corn chips or strips of sweet red pepper, jicama, and celery sticks.

8 cups cooked black beans and
   enough liquid to blend,
   about 2 cups
2-3 teaspoons salt
1/2 teaspoon dried coriander
1/4 teaspoon cayenne

3 jalapeno peppers, seeded
1 cup salsa, hot, med. or mild
1/4 cup lime juice
1/4 cup lemon juice
3 cloves garlic

Using the steel blade of a food processor, blend all the ingredients until the beans are fairly smooth, adding cooking liquid (up to 2 cups) as needed, to reach desired consistency. Don't overblend. We like some pieces of black bean to remain for aesthetic reasons.

Store black bean dip in the refrigerator, but serve at room temperature.

Black bean dip keeps two weeks refrigerated and also freezes well.

CHEESE AND GREEN CHILE DIP

Makes about 7 cups

What doesn't taste luscious with melted cheese? Cheese and Green Chile Dip works equally well with soy cheese. Nutritional information is based upon dairy cheese. Soy cheese is somewhat lower in fat and has no cholesterol.

tortilla chips	**1 can (4 ounces) green chiles, minced**
☐	
2 large white onions, minced	☐
2 large tomatoes, chopped	**1 pound cheddar or Monterey Jack cheese, grated**

Place tortilla chips on cookie sheets in the oven to warm.

Place chopped onions, tomato and green chiles in a frying pan. Simmer for 5 minutes over a low heat. Add cheese and cook gently for another five minutes.

Serve dip with warm tortilla chips.

DEBRA'S SALSA

Makes about 7 cups

A chunky and highly seasoned salsa, especially good on tacos or with chips. Try it on beans, fish, chicken or burritos.

2 large onions, chopped	1 teaspoon cumin
2 cloves garlic, chopped	1/2 teaspoon salt, optional
1 jalapeno pepper, seeded and minced	1/2 teaspoon black pepper
4 cups tomatoes, diced	1/4 teaspoon celery seed, optional
1 cup tomato puree	1/4 teaspoon basil
1 cup water	1/4 teaspoon oregano
1/2 tablespoon chili powder	2 tablespoons chopped parsley

Combine all the ingredients in a large stainless steel or enamel soup pot and simmer for 10 minutes.

This salsa keeps for several weeks when refrigerated.

ESCABECHE

Serves 12

Escabeche makes a great appetizer or main dish. Marinate overnight before serving. Escabeche keeps in the refrigerator for up to three weeks and improves with age!

1/2 cup fragrant green olive oil
2 pounds shelled and deveined shrimp (20-24 per pound)
☐
2 large onions, quartered and thinly sliced
6 cloves garlic, minced
2 medium carrots, halved and thinly sliced

2/3 cup apple cider or wine vinegar
2 bay leaves
1 teaspoon salt
1 teaspoon black pepper
1 teaspoon paprika

Gently warm olive oil in a large skillet and saute shrimp for two minutes, just until they turn pink. Transfer shrimp to a bowl.

Using the same skillet, saute onions, garlic and carrots for 5 minutes. Add vinegar, bay leaves, salt, pepper and paprika. Stir and cook for 2 minutes.

Pour vegetables with marinade over shrimp and mix lightly.

Cover and chill overnight.

HOUMOUS BI TAHINI

Makes 6 cups

Probably the best-known and best-loved Mid-East dish is houmous. Full of protein, calcium, fiber, and high in carbohydrates. Eat with pita and raw vegetables - what a meal!

4 cups cooked or canned chickpeas	1/2 cup lemon juice
1 cup tahini (sesame butter)	5 cloves garlic
1 cup liquid from beans	1-1/2 teaspoons salt
	dash cayenne pepper

Puree all ingredients using the steel blade of a food processor until the mixture moves freely under the blade and the garlic is well-incorporated. Add more liquid from beans if the mixture seems too stiff. Stop machine once or twice to scrape down the sides of the workbowl with a rubber spatula.

Cover and refrigerate houmous for several hours to give the flavors a chance to blend. Serve at room temperature.

Houmous keeps in the refrigerator for about a week. Store in the freezer for longer periods.

MARINATED MUSHROOMS

Makes about 8 cups

Quick and easy to make. Once the mushrooms are removed from the marinade, use to pickle more mushrooms or other vegetables such as zucchini spears.

2 pounds small mushrooms, cleaned and trimmed	**1 large onion, quartered**
☐	**1 tablespoon oregano**
1 cup cider vinegar	**1 teaspoon salt**
3 cloves garlic	**1 teaspoon black pepper**
	1 cup olive oil

Place mushrooms in a glass, ceramic, or stainless-steel bowl.

Using the steel blade of a food processor or a blender, blend garlic and onion with vinegar. Add blended mixture to mushrooms together with oregano, salt, pepper and olive oil.

Cover tightly and refrigerate overnight. Stir once or twice to make sure that the top mushrooms get turned under.

Remove mushrooms from the marinade with a slotted spoon. Delicious in tossed salads or serve as an appetizer.

NORI ROLLS

Serves 24

Dark, beautiful vegetarian sushi.

6 sheets toasted nori

2 cups raw Black Thai rice (a sticky rice)

4 cups water

1 package pickled sushi cucumbers, minced

1 package pickled sushi ginger, minced

1 tablespoon tahini

3 tablespoons tamari soy sauce

1 teaspoon black pepper

pinch cayenne pepper

2 carrots, grated

3 scallions, sliced

1 small jar pickled plum paste

Wasabi powder mixed with water to form paste

Bring water to a boil. Add rice, cover, lower heat, and simmer 45 minutes. Black Thai rice is sticky, which is perfect for this application. Allow rice to cool a little. When warm, mix with diced sushi cucumber, ginger, tahini, cayenne, black pepper, and soy sauce. Grate carrots and slice scallions, and set aside.

Place a dish of water on the work counter to moisten hands while working. Place a sheet of nori on work surface and lightly brush with pickled plum paste. Place 1/2 cup rice mixture on nori. Wet hands and pat rice to cover nori from side to side, leaving 1" at the top and 2" at the bottom. Sprinkle scallion and carrots near the bottom edge of the rice and roll the seaweed into a cigar-shaped cylinder. Cylinder should be firm and well-filled. Dampen outer edge of nori so it will stick when rolled.

When all sheets of nori are filled, slice each cylinder in 2" rounds using a sharp, wet knife. Arrange on a platter and serve with wasabi sauce for dipping.

PUMPKIN SEED–TOMATILLO DIP

Makes about 4 cups

A terrific party dip for tortilla chips, or a refreshing and low-calorie sauce for rice, beans, chicken or fish.

2 cups tomatillos, husked
□
1 cup pumpkin seeds
□
4 large garlic cloves
1/2 teaspoon dried coriander
2 jalapeno peppers, seeded
1/4 cup fresh parsley
2-1/2 tablespoons fresh lime juice

1/2 cup water
1 teaspoon salt
1 teaspoon black pepper
□
few tablespoons olive oil, optional
minced red onion as garnish

Place husked tomatillos in a pot with enough water to cover; bring to a boil, cook for 2 minutes and then drain.

Roast pumpkin seeds in a 350 degree oven on a cookie sheet for 4 minutes, until lightly toasted and fragrant, but still green. Cool.

Using the steel blade of a food processor and on/off turns, puree tomatillos, pumpkin seeds, garlic, coriander, jalapeno peppers, parsley, lime juice, water, salt and pepper. If desired, add a few tablespoons of olive oil.

Refrigerate if not using immediately. Dip keeps for a week in the refrigerator.

SMOKED SALMON MOUSSE

Makes 1-1/2 cups

Pipe this onto cucumber or pumpernickel rounds. Garnish with sprigs of fresh dill.

8 ounces natural cream cheese, room temperature
1/2 cup nonfat yogurt
4 ounces smoked salmon
1 tablespoon lemon juice
1 teaspoon dried dill weed

1/2 teaspoon black pepper
□
4 scallions, sliced, green and white parts
small sprigs of fresh dill

Blend cream cheese, yogurt, smoked salmon, lemon juice, dill weed and black pepper. Transfer to a bowl and stir in sliced scallions.

May also be used as a spread or dip.

STUFFED GRAPE LEAVES

Makes 36

Heavenly! The stuffing is wonderful in swiss chard or cabbage leaves too.

1 jar vine leaves (or about 36 fresh vine leaves, steamed until they turn a light green)	**1 cup raw rice (use Thai red, Wehani, or short-grain brown)**
□	**1/2 cup pine nuts (or chopped walnuts)**
4 tablespoons olive oil	**1/2 teaspoon salt**
2 medium onions, chopped	**1/2 teaspoon black pepper**
2 cloves garlic, minced	**1/4 cup lemon juice**
1 tablespoon dried parsley	**1-1/2 cups water**
□	□
1 teaspoon dried dill weed	**1/4 cup lemon juice**
1 teaspoon dried mint	**3/4 cup olive oil**

Remove vine leaves from jar and rinse with hot water in a colander. Drain well. Pat leaves dry. Place on linen towels with shiny side down.

Gently warm 4 tablespoons olive oil in a skillet. Saute onion, garlic, and parsley until onion is soft, about 2-3 minutes. Add dill, mint, rice and pine nuts. Saute 5 minutes. Rice will become fragrant. Add salt and pepper, 1/4 cup lemon juice, and the water. Cover and simmer for 40 minutes.

Cool rice mixture. When cool, place 2 teaspoons pilaf in the middle of the underside (not the shiny side) of the leaf near the stem. Roll grape leaves up egg-roll style by folding over the base side of the leaf (where the stem is attached), and folding in the sides. Roll tightly away from you.

continued . . .

STUFFED GRAPE LEAVES
(continued)

Arrange grape leaves in layers in an oven proof pot which has a heavy lid. Sprinkle each layer with a mixture of the remaining 1/4 cup lemon juice and 3/4 cup olive oil.

Weight the stuffed grape leaves with a plate. Cover. Bake in an 350 degree oven for 1/2 hour. When done baking, drain leaves and refrigerate. (Save oil and lemon mixture to use over other grains.) Serve grape leaves cold.

Some people like their grape leaves with yogurt.

If fresh leaves are used, you may want to increase the quantity of salt in the stuffing by 1/2 teaspoon.

Grape leaves store well in the refrigerator for about a week.

SUN-DRIED TOMATOES

Makes 3 cups

Delicious on pasta, rice or beans. Try sun-dried tomatoes on French bread as an appetizer.

6 ounces sun-dried tomatoes	**2 teaspoons dried basil**
1-1/2 cups apple cider vinegar	**1 teaspoon dried oregano**
❑	**1/2 teaspoon dried tarragon**
1-1/3 cups olive oil	**1/2 teaspoon dried thyme**
18 cloves garlic, sliced	**1/2 teaspoon dried marjoram**
12 whole black peppercorns	**1 teaspoon dried parsley**

Place tomatoes in a non-plastic or non-aluminum bowl. Heat vinegar in a stainless steel pot. Pour over tomatoes and let sit for 1 hour, stirring occasionally.

Drain tomatoes (save vinegar for use elsewhere).

Combine remaining ingredients in a large glass jar. Add tomatoes, stir and cover. Let tomatoes marinate for at least 24 hours.

Marinated tomatoes keep for several months. They may be stored for a longer period in the refrigerator, but bring to room temperature before serving.

WHITE BEAN–ROASTED GARLIC GREMOLATA

Makes 1-1/2 cups

A simplified gremolata. Serve with endive, radicchio leaves, carrot, fennel sticks and snow peas.

2 cups cooked cannellini (white kidney) beans	1/3 cup packed Italian flat parsley
1/4 cup lemon juice	1/2 teaspoon salt
1 tablespoon olive oil	1 teaspoon black pepper
6 cloves garlic	

Using the steel blade of a food processor, blend everything until smooth.

Transfer dip to a serving bowl and place vegetables around it.

Although this dip can be prepared a day ahead and refrigerated, bring to room temperature before serving.

Breads

Back at Kallimos . . .

We observed her closely as she spoke. She was a thin woman who stood perhaps five and a half feet tall. Her face bore the wrinkles that come with a lifetime of laughter and sunlight. Blue eyes sparkled at us as she spoke. Her thin lips curved into a smile easily, and a mane of brilliant white hair hung in a braid down her back. The most striking thing about her, though, was her dignity and poise. She moved and spoke with a quiet, unhurried confidence that made her easy to listen to—and to trust.

I noticed that her arms were well muscled for a woman of her age. She looked to be in her early seventies, though she clearly retained the better part of her youthful vigor.

The food and drink answered our hunger and thirst, but the act of consuming our meal left us immensely tired. The woman understood our fatigue and gently helped us back to bed. Then she drew a bench to the bedside and sat down.

continued . . .

"My name is Hannah. I will be watching over you as you regain your strength. In time, I will answer all of your questions, but now you must rest." She reached out and took Jude's hand in hers. "When you are stronger and the time is right, I will tell you about Kallimos."

Excerpted from Learning from Hannah © *William H. Thomas, M.D.*

7-GRAIN CEREAL BREAD

Makes 1 loaf   *Bake at 400*

1 tablespoon baking yeast	1/2 teaspoon salt
1 tablespoon honey	2 tablespoons flax seeds
1-1/4 cups warm water or milk	2 tablespoons brewer's yeast
□	(optional)
3 cups whole wheat flour	1/4 cup olive or sesame oil
1/2 cup 7-grain cereal	2 tablespoons cider vinegar

Using the steel blade of a food processor, combine yeast, honey and warm water. Let stand for 15 minutes until frothy.

Add the remaining ingredients and knead with the steel blade until the dough cleans the sides of the workbowl and appears smooth and pliable. If dough appears too dry, add water, 1 tablespoon at a time. If it appears too sticky, add 1 tablespoon of flour at a time.

Place dough in a bowl with 1 tablespoon oil and turn to coat. Cover with plastic wrap, or a shower cap, and let rise until doubled in bulk, about 50 minutes.

Grease bread pan. Punch down dough. Shape and put in pan. Cover and let bread rise again for another 50 minutes.

Preheat oven to 400 degrees. When bread is risen, bake 40 minutes, or until lightly browned. If bread sounds hollow when thumped on bottom, it's done.

Place bread pan on rack to cool for 10 minutes. Turn bread out from pan to finish cooling before slicing.

BEATRICE'S BASIC MUFFINS

Makes 12 muffins   *Bake at 350*

These muffins contain no baking powder. Baking powder is high in sodium and destroys some B-vitamins.

4 egg whites (yolks are in Group 3)

Group 1
> **1 cup sifted w/w pastry flour**
> **1/3 cup each wheat germ, bran and rolled oats**
> **1/4 cup powdered milk, optional**
> **pinch salt, optional**
> **pinch nutmeg or allspice, optional**
> **1/2 teaspoon cinnamon**

Group 2
> **1/2 cup raisins or chopped dates or other dried fruit**
> **1/2 cup chopped walnuts or pecans**

Group 3
> **1/2 cup yogurt or buttermilk**
> **1/2 cup apple juice**
> **1/2 cup applesauce or one banana or 1/2 cup grated carrot**
> **1/4 cup honey or molasses**
> **1 teaspoon vanilla**
> **4 egg yolks**

Using an electric mixer or hand beater, beat egg whites until stiff. Set aside.

Mix Group 1 ingredients in a large bowl. Place ingredients from Group 3 in blender and blend thoroughly. Stir liquid ingredients into dry.

continued . . .

BEATRICE'S BASIC MUFFINS
(continued)

Stir in Group 2 raisins (dates) and walnuts (pecans).

Fold in egg whites quickly using a rubber spatula.

Spoon muffin batter into 12 previously greased muffin wells. Bake at 350 degrees, approximately 30 minutes.

When baked, cool muffins in tins on racks for 10 minutes. Turn muffins out onto racks to finish cooling.

To make yeast muffins, soak a tablespoon or more of yeast in liquid ingredients and then add to dry. Proceed with rest of recipe.

Corn meal muffins can be made by using 1 cup corn meal and 1 cup wheat germ instead of whole wheat pastry flour and other dry ingredients. Honey is better than molasses in this recipe.

Try grinding sunflower seeds to replace some of the dry ingredients for another variation.

Rice polishings or other flour can be substituted for part of the whole wheat flour.

CARROT RAISIN TEA BREAD

Makes 2 loaves   *Bake at 325*

Wonderful with a cup of herbal tea. Try it toasted with almond or apple butter.

1 cup safflower or canola oil	3 cups w/w pastry flour
1 cup honey or fruit juice concentrate	2 teaspoons cinnamon
	1/2 teaspoon salt
3 eggs	1 teaspoon baking powder
1 tablespoon vanilla extract	1/2 teaspoon baking soda
3 cups grated carrot	□
	1 cup raisins

Preheat oven to 325 degrees.

Grease two 5x9 loaf pans.

In a large mixing bowl, whisk together oil, honey and eggs. Stir in vanilla and grated carrot.

In a second bowl, mix the dry ingredients. Stir into wet ingredients until moistened. Do not overmix. Fold in raisins.

Spoon batter into loaf pans.

Bake for 1 hour, or until a knife inserted into the center comes out clean. Remove pans from oven to cooling racks. Let stand for 10 minutes. Remove cakes from pans and finish cooling on racks.

CRANBERRY WALNUT MUFFINS

Makes 12 large muffins   *Bake at 375*

These make a wonderful addition to a holiday bread basket.

1-1/2 cups w/w pastry or spelt flour	2 eggs
2 teaspoons baking powder	1/2 cup sweet, sour or soy milk
1/2 teaspoon salt	□
1/2 teaspoon cinnamon	1 cup walnuts
3/4 cup honey or fruit concentrate	2 cups cranberries
1/4 cup safflower or canola oil	

Preheat oven to 375 degrees. Grease a muffin tin.

Blend all the ingredients, except walnuts and cranberries, using the steel blade of a food processor and on/off turns. Stop the machine once or twice to scrape down the sides of the workbowl with a rubber spatula.

Add walnuts and cranberries. Coarsely chop into the batter with several on/off turns.

Fill muffin wells 2/3 full. Bake muffins 30 minutes, or until lightly browned and springy to the touch.

Remove tin from oven and let stand 10 minutes before turning muffins out to finish cooling on a rack. Serve at room temperature, or store air-tight in the freezer. (If serving from the freezer, thaw still air-tight. Then, place muffins on cookie sheet and warm in a 375 degree oven for 5 minutes.)

CRISP SESAME BREADSTICKS

Makes 3 dozen   *Bake at 400*

These may be frozen and warmed on a cookie sheet before serving. Caraway seeds may be substituted for sesame seeds.

3-1/2 cups w/w bread flour or spelt flour	**1 tablespoon olive oil**
1 teaspoon salt	**1-1/4 cups warm water**
1 tablespoon baking yeast	□
	1/2 cup brown sesame seeds

Using the steel or plastic blade of a food processor, mix 1-1/2 cups of the flour, salt and yeast. With the machine running, pour in olive oil and warm water; process for 30 seconds.

Mix in sesame seeds. Gradually add enough of the remaining flour to make a soft, slightly sticky dough. Remove dough from workbowl and place in a bowl with 1 tablespoon oil. Turn dough to coat. Cover and let rise in a warm place until doubled in bulk, about one hour.

Punch down dough. Divide into 4 hunks and each hunk into 9 additional pieces. Form each piece into a cigar-shaped roll about 6 inches long. Place breadsticks on 3 greased baking sheets, 12 to a sheet, about an inch apart.

Cover baking sheets with a clean towel and let breadsticks rise in a warm place until doubled in bulk, about 30 minutes. While bread rises, preheat oven to 400 degrees.

Bake 20 minutes, or until golden brown. Cool on a rack.

DATE WALNUT MUFFINS

Makes 12 large muffins   *Bake at 400*

Great served with butter, peanut butter, or cream cheese for a quick weekend lunch.

2/3 cup w/w pastry flour	**1 cup chopped walnuts**
2/3 cup cornmeal	☐
1/3 cup bran	**2 eggs**
1/3 cup wheat germ	**1/4 cup safflower or soy oil**
1/2 teaspoon salt	**1/4 cup honey**
3 teaspoons baking powder	**1 cup sweet or sour milk**
1 cup date pieces in oat flour	

Preheat oven to 400 degrees.

Grease muffin tins.

Mix dry ingredients in a large bowl. Mix wet ingredients in a separate bowl. Combine wet and dry ingredients and mix briefly, just to moisten. Do not overmix or muffins will be tough.

Fill muffin wells 2/3 full and bake for 15-20 minutes, or until muffins are lightly browned and springy to the touch.

Take tin out of oven and cool on rack for 10 minutes before removing muffins.

They may be stored in the freezer and removed in the morning to stick into a lunchbox.

DATE WALNUT TEA CAKE

Makes one large loaf or 2 smaller ones   *Bake at 325*

Yummy with tea. For lunch, spread with nut butter.

1 cup w/w bread flour	*3/4 cup honey or fruit juice*
1 cup w/w pastry flour	*concentrate*
1/4 cup wheat germ	*2 eggs*
1/4 cup bran	*2 large, ripe bananas*
1/2 teaspoon salt	*2 tablespoons hot water*
1 teaspoon baking powder	□
1/4 cup safflower or canola	*1 cup walnuts*
oil	*1/2 cup date pieces in oat flour*

Preheat oven to 325 degrees. Grease a 9x5 loaf pan, or 2 mini loaf pans.

Blend all the ingredients, except walnuts and date pieces, using the steel blade of a food processor and on/off turns. Stop once or twice and scrape down the sides of the workbowl with a rubber spatula.

Add walnuts and date pieces and coarsely chop into batter with several on/off turns.

Fill prepared pan(s) with batter and bake 60-70 minutes, until bread is firm to touch and a knife inserted in the center comes out clean. When baked, cool in pan on rack for 10 minutes. Turn out and finish cooling on rack. Wrap tea cakes when completely cool.   Store a day before slicing.

HERB BREAD

Makes 1 loaf   *Bake at 350*

1/2 cup scalded milk   **1 egg**
2 tablespoons butter or olive oil   **1/2 teaspoon basil**
1 tablespoon honey   **1/2 teaspoon thyme**
1-1/2 teaspoons salt   **1 teaspoon oregano**
1/2 cup water   **2 teaspoons chives**
1 tablespoon baking yeast   **3-1/4 cups w/w flour**

Scald milk by bringing to a boil. When skin forms on top, combine milk with butter, honey and salt in a food processor using the steel blade. Cool to lukewarm by adding the water. Add yeast and mix with several on/off turns. Add egg, herbs and flour. Mix with several on/off turns. When dough forms a ball and cleans the workbowl, divide it into 7 or 8 smaller balls, press them around the blade, and process again for a second or two. Repeat this process twice.

Pour 1 tablespoon olive oil in bowl. Add dough, turning to coat, cover, and let rise until doubled in bulk, about 45 minutes. Punch down, shape dough into a loaf, place in a greased bread pan and let rise, covered, until double in bulk again, about 1 hour.

While bread rises, preheat oven to 350 degrees. Bake one hour.

When bread is baked, let stand in pan on rack for 10 minutes. Turn out on rack to finish cooling.

MOM'S BREAD

Makes 28 flat breads   *Bake at 350*

In 1962, our family dentist tore up his bill for $100 in exchange for 2 loaves of mom's bread. It's survival food! We make mom's bread in cookie form, which is easier to serve and eat.

1 teaspoon honey or barley malt	**1/3 cup rye flakes**
1 teaspoon molasses	**1/3 cup soy flakes**
2/3 cup warm water	**1/3 cup cornmeal**
2 tablespoons baking yeast	**1/3 cup seven-grain cereal**
☐	**2 tablespoons caraway seeds**
3 cups w/w bread flour	**1 teaspoon sea salt**
☐	**1/3 cup wheat, rice or oat**
1/2 cup barley flakes	**bran**
1/2 cup wheat flakes	**1/3 cup pumpkin seeds**
1/2 cup rolled oats	**1/3 cup sunflower seeds**
1/3 cup rice flakes	**1/3 cup sesame seeds**
1/3 cup flax seeds	☐
1/3 cup millet	**2-3 cups warm water**

Grains and flours should be at room temperature.

Pour 2/3 cup hot water over sweeteners in a large jar or bowl. When water cools to lukewarm, add yeast and stir to dissolve. Place mixture in a warm, draft-free location until the mixture is foamy.

Place flour in large mixing bowl. Using the steel blade of a food processor, blend all grains, flakes and seeds. Some grains, like millet, will remain almost whole, so don't expect the mixture to be smooth. Add grains to flour in bowl and mix. Then

continued . . .

MOM'S BREAD
(continued)

add yeast mixture. Gradually stir in 2-3 glasses of warm water, just enough so dough will hold together.

Grease baking sheets. Place mom's bread, roughly 1/3 cup dough per bread, on baking sheets about 3 inches apart to allow room for rising. Flatten each slightly with the palm of the hand. If using an electric oven, warm to 200 degrees and turn off before putting breads in to rise for 15 minutes. If using gas, put baking sheets in a turned-off oven and let breads rise for the same amount of time.

When batter has risen, turn oven to 350 degrees and bake until rolls are lightly browned, about 30 minutes. Remove to cooling racks.

We like to toast mom's bread until nice and brown. However, when cool, it is like hard-tack, great to take hiking or on vacations because it will not mold.

MOM'S SESAME CORNCRISPS

Makes about 24   *Bake at 400*

Homely, but corncrisps taste great and don't last long!

1 cup boiling water	**2 tablespoons corn or**
□	**peanut oil**
1 cup coarse cornmeal	**1/2 teaspoon salt**
7/8 cup brown sesame seeds	

Preheat oven to 400 degrees.

Bring water to a boil. Combine cornmeal, sesame seeds, oil and salt in a bowl and pour over boiling water. Stir until smooth.

Grease two cookie sheets. Onto cookie sheets, drop corncrisps by tablespoonfuls close together. They don't spread. Flatten crisps using your fingers.

Bake 20 minutes, or until golden brown around the edges. Remove corncrisps with a metal spatula to cool on a wire rack.

Serve with soups, salad, or guacamole. If any crisps remain, store airtight in freezer. Reheat to crisp.

NEW ORLEANS BLACK MUFFINS

Makes 12 large muffins   *Bake at 350*

Serve these aromatic muffins warm. Best eaten the same day.

2 cups roasted pecans
□
3/4 cup hot water
1/2 cup molasses
1/4 cup sweet, sour or
**   or soy milk**

3 cups w/w pastry flour or
**   spelt flour**
3/4 cup honey
2 teaspoons baking powder
1 teaspoon salt

Roast pecans on a cookie sheet in a 300 degree oven for 10 minutes. Coarsely chop using the steel blade of a food processor. Remove nuts from workbowl and set aside.

Preheat oven to 350 degrees.

Line 12-cup muffin tin with paper liners or grease muffin wells.

Using the steel blade of the food processor again, blend all the ingredients, except for the pecans, until the batter moves freely under the blade.

Add pecans and mix in with three quick on/off turns.

Divide batter among muffin wells. Bake for 25 minutes, or until nicely browned. Remove muffin tin from the oven and let stand for 5-10 minutes. Transfer muffins to rack and cool.

PEPPER ANISEED CRACKERBREAD

Makes 10   *Bake at 450*

Pepper aniseed crackerbread is best eaten the day it is made. Good with soups and salads.

2 cups w/w or spelt flour   **1 tablespoon barley malt**
1 teaspoon aniseed   **syrup**
1 teaspoon coarse black pepper   **1/2 cup water**
1 teaspoon salt   **1/4 cup olive or safflower oil**

Blend flour, aniseed, pepper and salt using the steel blade of a food processor. While the machine is running, add barley malt, water and oil. Process until a ball forms and cleans the workbowl, about 15-20 seconds. The dough will be smooth. Cover workbowl with plastic or a clean shower cap. Let dough rest 15 minutes. (Can be prepared 1 day ahead and refrigerated.)

Preheat oven to 450 degrees. Grease a baking sheet.

Divide dough into 10 pieces. Work with 2 pieces of dough at a time, making sure remaining pieces are covered to prevent drying out.

Using a rolling pin, roll the 2 pieces into thin 8-inch rounds, like a pizza crust. Arrange on the baking sheet. Bake until light brown, about 8 minutes. Remove crackerbreads to cool on a rack.

Continue the same way with the remainder of the dough.

PEPPERY BREAD WREATH

Makes 1 bread wreath   *Bake at 350*

1 tablespoon baking yeast
1-1/2 cups warm water
          ☐
2-1/2 cups w/w pastry flour
1 cup w/w bread flour
1/4 cup olive oil
1 teaspoon salt

1 tablespoon black pepper
1 tablespoon dried rosemary
1/4 cup brown sesame seeds
1/4 cup poppy seeds
          ☐
1 egg yolk beaten with
   milk or water as a glaze

Sprinkle yeast over warm water in the workbowl of a food processor. Using the steel blade, stir to dissolve. Let stand 10 minutes until foamy.

To the workbowl, add flours, olive oil, salt, black pepper, rosemary, and half the sesame and poppy seeds. Knead for a minute with on/off turns, until dough cleans the sides of the workbowl and appears smooth and elastic. Add a tablespoon more flour if dough appears too sticky; add a tablespoon water if it appears too dry. Don't overprocess as the heat of the motor will kill the yeast.

Pour 2 tablespoons olive oil into a large bowl. Add dough, turning to coat. Cover bowl with plastic wrap, or a shower cap, and let dough rise until doubled in bulk, about 1 hour.

Grease a cookie sheet. Punch down dough. Cut into 8 pieces. Form each into a ball and roll in remaining sesame and poppy seeds. Arrange balls in a ring on the cookie sheet, flattening slightly so they touch and form a wreath. Cover with a towel and place in a warm draft-free spot. Let rise until doubled in bulk again, about 35 minutes.

continued . . .

PEPPERY BREAD WREATH
(continued)

Preheat oven to 350 degrees.

Bake wreath 20 minutes. Brush with egg yolk and water as glaze and continue baking until bread is golden and sounds hollow when tapped on bottom, about 10 minutes.

Remove bread from oven and cool on rack.

Best served the same day it is made. The pepper in this bread gives it a little unexpected kick.

SOFT CARAWAY BREADSTICKS

Makes 1 dozen long breadsticks   *Bake at 425*

1 tablespoon baking yeast   □
1/2 cup lukewarm water   **1 egg**
1 teaspoon honey   □
□   **3-1/2 cups w/w pastry**
1/2 cup safflower or canola oil   **flour, approximately**
1-1/2 tablespoons honey   **2 tablespoons caraway**
1 teaspoon salt   **seeds, more at end**
1/2 cup boiling water   **1 egg, with 1 teaspoon water**

Sprinkle yeast over water and whisk until yeast is dissolved. Add 1 teaspoon honey. Stir again.

Using the plastic or steel blade of a food processor, mix the oil, 1-1/2 tablespoons honey, salt and boiling water. When this cools to lukewarm, add egg and yeast mixture. Whirl again. Add flour, one cup at a time, mixing several seconds after each addition. Add caraway seeds. Blend briefly, with on/off turns of processor, but do not knead.

Refrigerate workbowl until the dough is chilled and firm.

Grease cookie sheet. Divide dough into 12 pieces. On a floured board and in your hands, roll dough into breadsticks about a foot in length. Place 1-2" apart on the baking sheet and brush with beaten egg/water. Lightly press additional caraway seeds into breadsticks. Let rise uncovered about 30 minutes.

While breads rise, preheat oven to 425 degrees. Bake 15 minutes. Remove breadsticks from cookie sheet to cool on rack.

SUNFLOWER SPICE APPLE MUFFINS

Makes 12 large muffins   *Bake at 375*

Really small cakes. Frosted, they can be used for birthday parties.

2 cups w/w pastry flour	2 teaspoons baking powder
1/2 cup wheat germ	□
1 cup sunflower seeds	1/2 cup canola or
2 cups dried apple pieces	safflower oil
1/2 teaspoon salt	1 cup honey or fruit concentrate
1 teaspoon allspice	5 eggs
1 teaspoon cinnamon	2 teaspoons vanilla
1/4 cup powdered dry milk	1/4 cup water

Preheat oven to 375 degrees.

Grease muffin tins.

Mix dry ingredients in a large bowl. Mix wet ingredients in a separate bowl. Combine wet and dry ingredients and mix briefly, enough to moisten batter. Do not overmix or muffins will be tough.

Fill muffin wells 2/3 full and bake for 15-20 minutes, or until muffins are lightly browned and springy to the touch.

Remove tin from oven and let stand 10 minutes before removing muffins to a cooling rack.

These muffins keep for a week in the refrigerator and freeze nicely too.

Soups

Back at Kallimos . . .

Hannah leaned forward and set her chin in her hands. Her voice dropped almost to a whisper. "I don't know how to tell you this. I doubt you will believe me when you hear

continued . . .

the truth about your situation." The change in her manner set Jude and me on edge. "No one knows how or why it happens, but on very rare occasions strangers appear on the shore of Kallimos. People say the strangers come from the Other World. I, like you, came here from the Other World. I was just nine years old when I arrived. My father was a physician, and we lived in Norfolk, Virginia. He was a skillful sailor and he loved the sea. Each winter, we took our holiday among the islands of the Caribbean. Our boat was destroyed as yours was, and the cold, dark water you describe pulled me from my mother's arms."

Tears welled in Hannah's eyes. She paused for a moment and then continued. "A woman named Haleigh, whom you will meet, took me in and raised me. She helped me grieve for my lost life and the death of my parents. Being with you reminds me of the life I lost that day. But since the days of the ancients, no one from the Other World has ever returned to it. There is no way back. . . .

. . . "The pain of your loss is great. But I can assure you that, in time, you will know the ways of the people of Kallimos and become part of this world. Fate has given you this life, both of you. Now you both must learn how to live it."

Excerpted from Learning from Hannah © *William H. Thomas, M.D.*

CAULIFLOWER SOUP WITH BASIL AND PINE NUTS

Serves 8

A fragrant, blended soup. Serve with herb bread slathered with pesto. Ripe tomatoes on the side and fresh peaches for dessert.

2 tablespoons pine nuts	**8 cups water or vegetable stock**
□	□
1 small head cauliflower, broken into florets	**1 teaspoon dried basil**
1 potato, cubed	**2 tablespoons olive oil**
2 onions, quartered	**salt and pepper to taste**
	1/2 cup watercress leaves, for garnish

Toast pine nuts in the oven at 300 degrees for 10 minutes. Remove from oven and set aside to cool.

Steam cauliflower florets, potato and onions in a large pot with 2 cups water until vegetables are tender, about 20 minutes.

Using a food processor or blender, blend soup. Add liquid as needed so soup flows under the blade smoothly. Return soup to kettle and add remaining water, basil and olive oil.

Season to taste with salt and pepper. Gently reheat.

Ladle into bowls. Garnish with watercress leaves and toasted pine nuts. Serve immediately.

CHICKEN SOUP WITH HERBS

Serves 4-6

A classic comfort soup. Good for what ails you.

2 carrots, diced
6 cloves garlic, minced
1 tablespoon dried parsley
6 cups chicken broth (or
   vegetable stock)
1/4 cup raw kasha (buckwheat
   groats)
1/2 cup soup noodles

2 cups diced boneless chicken,
   either cooked or raw
1/2 teaspoon oregano
1/2 teaspoon thyme
1/2 teaspoon tarragon
1/2 teaspoon black pepper
1/2 teaspoon cayenne pepper
salt to taste

Place ingredients, except salt, in a large kettle. Bring soup to a boil. Cover and simmer for 20 minutes, or until kasha is cooked and noodles are soft.

Season to taste with salt. Serve immediately.

Chicken broth can be made by cooking the carcass of a chicken with enough water to cover bones for 2-3 hours over low heat. Use turkey bones the same way.

After Thanksgiving, making turkey stock is a great way to get the bones out of the refrigerator. Make stock in large quantities and freeze in glass jars for use during the coming months. Be sure to allow room for expansion when freezing stock.

COLD BEET BORSCHT

Serves 6

Cold borscht, a hot potato in the bowl, and a dollop of yogurt or sour cream make a cooling summer soup. The pink broth is a perfect backdrop for hard boiled eggs and lemon slices.

6 medium beets, grated
1 large onion, quartered
1-1/2 quarts water
1 tablespoon salt
2 tablespoons lemon juice
1/4 cup honey

6 boiled potatoes
3 hard-boiled eggs, quartered
1 small lemon, thinly sliced
sour cream or yogurt
watercress or parsley for
** garnish**

Using the grating disk of a food processor, grate beets and onion. Place beets and onion in a soup kettle. Add water and salt and bring to a boil. Turn heat off and let pot sit, covered, for 10 minutes.

Stir in lemon juice and honey. (Lemon juice will return color to beets.) Cool soup, then refrigerate until cold, about 3 hours.

To serve, put a hot potato in each soup bowl and ladle borscht over potato. A dollop of sour cream or yogurt gets stirred in. Two egg quarters, a few lemon slices, and a sprinkling of watercress leaves or chopped parsley give the final touch.

COLD FRUIT SOUP

Serves 8

Serve this rosy soup cold. It hits the spot when it's too hot to eat.

1-1/2 quarts water
1/2 orange, sliced thinly
1/2 cup raisins
1/2 cup pineapple dices
1/3 cup honey
2 tablespoons arrowroot
□
1 cup blueberries

1 cup sliced peaches
1 cup cherries, pitted
2 tablespoons lemon juice
1 teaspoon orange extract
1 teaspoon lemon extract
dash cinnamon
dash ginger

Combine water, orange, raisins, pineapple, honey and arrowroot in a large kettle. Simmer soup 20 minutes. Remove kettle from stove and cool soup until barely warm - about 30 minutes.

Add remaining ingredients, mix thoroughly, and refrigerate until very cold.

CORN CHOWDER

Serves 6-8

Ah, the aroma of olive oil warming in a pot! This chowder is thick and wonderful.

2 tablespoons olive oil	3 cups corn kernels,
1 large onion, chopped	fresh or frozen
2 ribs celery, chopped	1 tablespoon dried parsley
1/2 green pepper, chopped	☐
2 large potatoes, diced	2 cups milk or soy milk
2 cups water or vegetable stock	1 teaspoon black pepper
1/2 teaspoon turmeric	1 teaspoon salt
1 bay leaf	

Gently warm olive oil in a large kettle. Saute onion and celery until soft, but not browned. Add green pepper, potato, water, turmeric and bay leaf. Bring soup to a boil. Cover pot, lower heat, and simmer 15 minutes, or until potatoes are tender when pierced with a knife.

Add corn and parsley and simmer another 3-5 minutes.

Remove bay leaf. Using a food processor or blender, blend half the soup to give it body. Return soup to kettle. Stir in milk. Heat soup, but do not bring to a boil or milk will curdle.

Add salt and pepper to taste, stir, and serve.

CUBAN BLACK BEAN SOUP

Serves 6-8

Black turtle beans accented with garlic, oregano, cumin, and cayenne pepper.

3 cups dried black beans
☐
1/4 cup olive oil
2 large onions, chopped
1/2 medium green pepper, chopped
☐
1 tablespoon dried parsley
4 cloves garlic, minced
1/2 teaspoon oregano

1/2 teaspoon cumin
1/4 teaspoon cayenne pepper
12 cups water or stock
1 teaspoon salt
1 teaspoon black pepper
☐
lemon juice, optional
jalapeno, minced, optional
☐
red onion chopped for garnish

Rinse and sort black beans for small stones. Black beans have more than their share!

Gently warm olive oil in a large kettle. Saute onions and green pepper until soft.

Add parsley, garlic, beans, oregano, spices and water to kettle and bring soup to a boil. Cover pot, lower heat, and simmer until beans are soft and soup begins to thicken, about 1-2 hours. Add salt and pepper.

Using a food processor or blender, blend half the soup. Leave the other half unblended to vary texture. Return blended soup to kettle. Taste and adjust seasoning.

For a tangy version, add lemon juice; for more heat, add minced jalapeno pepper. Garnish with chopped red onion.

CURRIED SWEET POTATO SOUP

Serves 6-8

A vibrantly colored soup with a hint of Asia.

2 tablespoons olive oil
1 large onion, chopped
2 cloves garlic, minced
1/2 teaspoon cumin
1/2 teaspoon coriander
1/2 teaspoon cinnamon
1/2 teaspoon ginger

1/4 teaspoon cayenne
1/2 teaspoon turmeric
2 teaspoons salt
☐
about 7 sweet potatoes, cut into chunks, assorted sizes fine
5 cups water or vegetable stock
lemon juice, optional

Gently warm olive oil in a large kettle and saute onions and garlic until soft. Add remaining spices and stir a minute or two until fragrant.

Add sweet potatoes and water to kettle and simmer until potatoes are easily pierced by a knife. Using a food processor or blender, blend soup until no lumps of potato remain.

Return soup to kettle and warm. Taste and adjust seasoning. Add more cayenne if desired. For tartness, add lemon.

GAZPACHO

Serves 12

The flavors of Spain, Portugal, and Mexico in a spicy, cold tomato soup. Best with fresh, ripe tomatoes, but diced, canned ones work fine.

12 large tomatoes, diced
2 pickling cucumbers
1 green pepper
2 cloves garlic
1 small onion

2 jalapeno peppers, seeded
pinch each dried parsley, basil,
thyme, oregano
1/4 cup lemon juice
1 teaspoon salt, optional

Place half the diced tomatoes in a large bowl or soup pot or glass jar. Using a food processor or blender, blend remaining tomatoes, cucumber, green pepper, garlic, onion and jalapeno peppers. Stir blended mixture into diced tomatoes. Stir in herbs and lemon juice.

Taste and adjust seasoning by adding a pinch of black pepper or more lemon. Serve very cold garnished with a sprig of parsley or watercress.

If tomatoes are too liquidy and soup needs body, add a spoonful of tomato puree.

INDIAN YELLOW SPLIT PEA SOUP

Serves 8-10

In this soup, yellow lentils meld perfectly with cumin, tomato and rice.

2 tablespoons olive oil	**2 cups chopped tomatoes**
2 large onions, chopped	**1/4 cup dried parsley**
2 teaspoons cumin	**2 dried chiles, stemmed,**
☐	**seeded and crumbled**
3 cups yellow split peas	**2 cups cooked Basmati rice**
12 cups water or stock	**1 teaspoon salt**
1 teaspoon turmeric	**☐**
	pepper to taste

Gently warm olive oil in a large kettle. Add chopped onion and saute until translucent. Add cumin and stir for one minute until fragrant.

Add split peas, water and turmeric to kettle. Bring soup to a boil, cover pot, and simmer until peas are soft, about an hour.

Add tomato, parsley, chiles, rice, and salt. Simmer for another 15 minutes.

Taste and season with pepper before serving.

INDONESIAN PEANUT BUTTER SOUP

Serves 8-10

Strange combination? No, a winner!

2 tablespoons olive oil
4 cloves garlic, minced
1 tablespoon grated fresh
   ginger root
2 cups diced onions
2 green peppers, diced
   ☐
3 cups water or vegetable stock
3 cups chunky natural, unsalted
   peanut butter

1/2 teaspoon cayenne
   ☐
1 pound spinach or swiss
   chard, coarsely chopped
1 tablespoon fresh lemon juice
4 cups milk or soy milk
salt to taste

Gently warm olive oil in a large kettle. Saute garlic and ginger, stirring until garlic is tender and ginger is fragrant. Add onions and peppers and saute for 5 minutes, until peppers are brightly colored.

Using a food processor or blender, blend peanut butter and water. Whisk mixture into soup, together with cayenne. Simmer 15 minutes.

Remove soup from heat, add spinach, lemon juice and milk. Stir, cover, and let soup stand 10 minutes to give the flavors a chance to blend.

Taste, adjust seasoning and serve.

LENTIL SOUP WITH BROWN RICE

Serves 6-8

Simple and simply superb!

2 cups dried lentils
1/2 cup raw brown rice
10 cups water or vegetable stock
6 cloves garlic, minced
4 carrots, diced
1 cup tomato juice
1 cup diced tomatoes
2 tablespoons dried parsley

1/2 teaspoon celery seed,
** optional**
□
1/2 teaspoon salt
1 teaspoon black pepper
2 cups shredded, dark green
** leafy vegetables**

Place lentils, rice, water, garlic, carrots, tomato juice, tomatoes and herbs in a soup kettle and bring soup to a boil. Lower heat, cover pot, and simmer until lentils are soft and rice is tooth-tender, about an hour.

Season to taste with salt and pepper. Add green leafy vegetables, cover pot and let soup stand 5-10 minutes. Serve immediately and watch it disappear!

LENTIL SOUP WITH RICE AND APRICOTS

Serves 8-10

Apricots in lentil soups are not unusual in the Middle East, Asia or Russia. They lend a sweetness and thickness to soup. Garnish with minced parsley.

2 tablespoons olive oil
1 large onion, chopped
6 cloves garlic, minced
☐
1/2 cup raw brown rice
1 green pepper, chopped
1/4 teaspoon cinnamon
1/4 teaspoon cayenne
1 tablespoon paprika
2 tablespoons dried parsley

1 tablespoon chopped fresh mint, optional
2 cups dried lentils
10 cups water or vegetable stock
1 cup chopped dried apricots
☐
1 teaspoon salt
1 teaspoon black pepper

Gently warm olive oil in a soup kettle. Saute onion and garlic until onion is translucent. Add rice and pepper. Stir until rice is coated with oil. Add remaining ingredients (except salt and pepper) and simmer, covered, until lentils and rice are cooked, about 1 hour.

Season to taste with salt and pepper before serving.

MEDITERRANEAN FISH SOUP WITH WHITE BEANS

Serves 6-8

An easy chowder. As with so many hearty soups, serve with crusty brown bread and a green salad for a complete meal.

1/4 cup olive oil
2 large onions, chopped
2 cloves garlic, minced
2 cups chopped tomatoes
1 bay leaf
1 teaspoon thyme
1/2 teaspoon basil
1 teaspoon grated orange peel
2 tablespoons dried parsley

1/2 teaspoon black pepper
1/2 teaspoon cayenne pepper
6 cups water or fish stock
□
2 cups cooked white beans
1 pound mild white fish (such as haddock) cut into 1-inch pieces
1/2 cup lemon juice
chopped parsley for garnish

Gently warm olive oil in a kettle. Saute onions and garlic until soft. Add tomatoes, bay leaf, thyme, basil, orange peel, parsley, pepper, cayenne pepper and 6 cups water. Bring soup to a boil.

Add the cooked beans, fish and lemon juice to soup. Simmer 10 minutes. Taste and adjust seasoning. Sprinkle with parsley and serve.

Leftover cooked rice or potatoes can be used in place of beans.

MOLDAVIAN VEGETABLE SOUP

Serves 6

Light and satisfying. Serve with corn bread and a salad of ripe red tomatoes, olives, and feta cheese.

1 large onion, chopped	2 tablespoons dried parsley
5 cloves garlic, minced	1 teaspoon dried dill weed
2 carrots, halved lengthwise and sliced	1 teaspoon thyme
	1/2 teaspoon marjoram
1 rib celery, sliced	2 bay leaves
1 large green pepper, chopped	dash cayenne pepper
3 large potatoes, diced	1 teaspoon black pepper
2 cups chopped tomatoes	1 teaspoon salt
2 cups fresh or frozen corn	6 cups water or vegetable stock
1/3 cup kasha (buckwheat groats)	

Place all ingredients in a large kettle and bring soup to a boil. Lower heat and simmer, covered, about 30 minutes.

Taste and adjust seasoning before serving.

MUSHROOM BARLEY SOUP

Serves 6

Thick and creamy with barley. Inspired by the earthy aroma of mushrooms.

1 cup barley	1 tablespoon dried dill seed
3 cups water	2 tablespoons dried parsley
☐	6 cups water or vegetable stock
1/2 cup dried mushrooms	2 bay leaves
(Formosan is nice)	1 teaspoon black pepper
1 large onion, chopped	☐
2 cloves garlic, chopped	salt to taste
1 pound carrots, diced	dash cayenne pepper

In a large kettle, bring 3 cups water to a boil. Add barley. Bring water to a second boil, cover pot and turn heat to low. Allow barley to simmer for 45 minutes.

Add remaining ingredients, except salt and cayenne, to kettle. Simmer soup another hour.

Season with salt and cayenne to taste before serving.

Mushroom barley is even better the second and third days. However, warm gently and add more water as needed. Barley soaks it up!

PEASANT MINESTRONE SOUP

Serves 12

A meal in itself. Thick and chunky, popular, hard to resist.

10 cloves garlic, chopped	1/2 cup pitted green olives, halved
1 red onion, diced	
1 cup dried white beans	1 bay leaf
4 carrots, halved lengthwise and sliced	1 teaspoon oregano
	1 teaspoon basil
2 ribs celery, sliced	1/2 teaspoon cayenne pepper
6 cups water or vegetable stock	8 ounces noodles or other pasta
☐	
2 cups tomato puree	☐
1 cup diced tomato	1/2 pound spinach or swiss chard, coarsely chopped

Add garlic, onion, beans, carrots, celery and water to kettle. Bring soup to a boil. Cover pot, lower heat, and simmer until beans are tender, about 1-1/2 hours.

Add tomato puree, tomato, olives, bay leaf, oregano, basil and cayenne. Add pasta to soup. Cover and simmer 15 minutes.

Stir in green leafy vegetable. Taste and adjust seasoning before serving with chunks of fresh brown bread.

PEASANT POTATO SOUP

Serves 8-10

A simple, old-fashioned potato-onion soup from my mother, Beatrice Stark. The flecks of potato peel make this soup look gourmet!

10 large potatoes, unpeeled, quartered
5 large onions, quartered

10 cups water or stock
1 teaspoon salt
1 teaspoon black pepper

Place potatoes and onions in a kettle with barely enough water to cover. Bring to a boil. Cover pot and simmer soup until potatoes are easily pierced with a knife, about 15 minutes.

Take a second kettle and place next to food processor. From the first kettle, remove potatoes and onions in batches to blend. Add liquid from pot as needed so that potato-onion mixture flows under the blade smoothly. As each batch is blended, place in the second kettle.

Add no more water than necessary. Soup should be the consistency of light cream. When soup is blended, stir in salt and pepper. Taste and adjust as needed.

For a richer version of this soup, add a little butter or olive oil.

PEA SOUP WITH RED LENTILS AND BARLEY

Serves 12-14

A bowl of steaming soup that's heaven to come home to on a cold day. The longer it stands, the thicker and better it gets. Thin with water or vegetable broth if serving on the second or third day.

1 large onion, diced	*2 stalks celery, diced*
5 cloves garlic, minced	*1 teaspoon cumin*
3 cups dried mixed yellow and green split peas	*1 teaspoon marjoram*
3/4 cup red lentils	*18 cups water or vegetable stock*
3/4 cup barley	*□*
4 carrots, diced	*salt and pepper to taste*

Add all ingredients except salt and pepper to kettle. Stir and bring to a boil. Lower heat, cover pot, and simmer until peas and barley are tender, about 2-1/2 hours.

Season with salt and pepper to taste before serving.

POTATO DUMPLINGS

Makes 24 dumplings

Turn vegetable or chicken broth into something special with piping hot potato dumplings!

2 large potatoes, boiled soft, skin left on	**1 teaspoon salt**
1/4 cup hot water, or vegetable stock	**3 tablespoons olive oil or chicken fat**
1/2 teaspoon garlic powder	**3 eggs**
1/4 teaspoon oregano	**1 cup matzo meal or whole wheat flour**
1/4 teaspoon thyme	**☐**
1/4 teaspoon cayenne pepper	**parsley or watercress, for garnish**

4 quarts vegetable or chicken broth

Blend all ingredients, except 4 quarts liquid, using the steel blade of a food processor, or mash potatoes with potato masher and mix in remaining ingredients using a wooden spoon.

Chill dumpling batter several hours.

Bring the 4 quarts vegetable or chicken broth to a boil. Drop dumplings by tablespoonfuls into broth. Cover and simmer 20 minutes.

Ladle broth into bowls and give everyone two or three potato dumplings. Garnish with chopped parsley or watercress leaves.

RED LENTIL SOUP WITH GINGER

Serves 10

Even if you don't like ginger, you'll love this soup!

4 cups red lentils
1 tablespoon fresh ginger,
  minced
1 pound carrots, diced
3 large onions, chopped
4 stalks celery, sliced

12 cups water or stock
1/2 cup dried parsley
□
1 teaspoon salt
1 teaspoon black pepper

Place ingredients, except salt and pepper, in a large soup kettle and bring to a boil. Lower heat, cover pot, and simmer for an hour.

Season to taste with salt and pepper before serving.

ROASTED PECAN SOUP WITH RED BELL PEPPER

Serves 4

Pecans, potatoes, and roasted red bell pepper. A wonderful, rich party soup.

2 tablespoons olive oil	**1 tablespoon lemon juice**
1 onion, chopped	**1 cup roasted, ground**
1 clove garlic, minced	**pecans or pecan meal**
☐	**salt and pepper to taste**
4 large potatoes, diced	☐
4-1/2 cups water	**1 small red bell pepper**
☐	**2/3 cup milk or soy milk**

Gently warm olive oil in a large kettle. Saute onion and garlic until slightly brown. Add potato and 2 cups water. Cover pot and simmer soup for 10-15 minutes, or until potatoes can be pierced easily with a knife. Add more water if needed so potato does not stick to bottom of pot or burn.

Using a food processor or blender, blend soup. Stir in lemon juice, ground pecans, and salt and pepper to taste. Let soup sit covered while proceeding with remaining ingredients.

Roast red pepper under a broiler until the skin is charred. Rinse under cold water and remove stalk, seeds and outer skin. Mash finely and whisk in milk or soy milk.

Heat soup and serve in bowls with red bell pepper mixture spooned on top.

RUSSIAN BORSCHT

Serves 10-12

There are many variations of borscht. This is our interpretation of borscht made for us by Rita Bykovsky. Serve hot or cold.

6 carrots, grated
6 beets, grated
1 large onion, chopped
2 cups diced tomatoes
3 small potatoes, diced
1 sweet green pepper, diced
1 small apple, diced
1/2 head cabbage, shredded
1 cup fresh mushrooms, sliced
1 yellow squash, quartered
   lengthwise and sliced

1/4 cup cider vinegar or
   lemon juice
1 bay leaf
1/4 cup dried parsley leaves
2 teaspoons dried dill weed
4 whole peppercorns
4 tablespoons honey
2 quarts water
   ❑
salt to taste
yogurt or sour cream, garnish
chopped scallions, for garnish

Using the grating disk of a food processor, grate carrots and beets. Prepare the remaining vegetables and combine all ingredients in a large soup kettle. Simmer 1-1/2 hours.

Taste and adjust seasoning. Serve borscht with a dollop of yogurt or sour cream and a sprinkle of sliced scallions.

Borscht tastes better the second day. So, let it sit overnight in the refrigerator if you can. If you must serve it the day it is made, let borscht sit for several hours to give the flavors a chance to blend.

SAVORY TOMATO RICE SOUP WITH HERBED YOGURT

Serves 10

A hint of orange and generous pinches of herbs bring this tomato rice soup alive! Delicious cold too.

2 tablespoons olive oil
1/2 teaspoon orange peel
1 large onion, chopped
4 cloves garlic, chopped
□
1 tablespoon dried basil
1 teaspoon marjoram
1 teaspoon cumin
pinch cayenne pepper
□
4 cups diced tomatoes

1 cup tomato puree
2-3 cups water or vegetable broth
2 cups cooked brown rice
salt and pepper to taste
□
Herbed Yogurt, optional
1 cup plain no-fat yogurt
1 bunch scallions, sliced
1 tablespoon dried basil
1/2 teaspoon garlic powder

Gently warm olive oil in a large kettle. Add orange peel, onions and garlic, and saute until onions are soft, about 5 minutes.

Stir in herbs, cumin and cayenne pepper. Cook until cumin is fragrant, about 5 minutes. Add tomatoes, tomato puree, water and cooked rice, and bring soup to boil. Reduce heat to low, cover pot, and simmer 10 minutes.

Taste and adjust seasoning. For herbed yogurt, whisk ingredients together. Place a dollop in each bowl to serve.

SOUR CHERRY AND YOGURT SUMMER SOUP

Serves 4

A tart, refreshing cherry soup. Chill thoroughly before serving. Garnish with pitted whole cherries and almond slivers.

2 cups plain low-fat yogurt	□
1/2 pound pitted fresh cherries	*several pitted whole cherries for*
1/4 teaspoon almond extract	*garnish*
1/4 cup fruit sweetener or honey	*almond slivers, optional*

Using a food processor or blender, blend yogurt, cherries, almond extract and sweetener. Flecks of fruit make the soup more attractive, so don't overblend!

Chill 4 hours or overnight before garnishing and serving.

One can substitute peaches, apricots, or even strawberries for cherries.

SPICY CURRIED ZUCCHINI SOUP

Serves 6

A fragrant, spicy soup which makes the kitchen smell irresistible.

2 tablespoons olive oil
1 large onion, chopped
2 cloves garlic, chopped
1 apple, chopped
☐
2 teaspoons curry powder
1/2 teaspoon cayenne pepper
☐
2 cups water or vegetable stock

1 cup cooked Basmati or
   brown rice
4 small-medium zucchini
☐
1 quart milk or soy milk
☐
salt and pepper to taste
pumpkin seeds for garnish

Gently warm olive oil in a large kettle. Saute onion, garlic, and apple until soft and fragrant. Sprinkle with curry and cayenne. Stir a few seconds.

Add water and bring soup to a boil. Add cooked rice and zucchini. Simmer 10 minutes until zucchini are easily pierced with a knife.

Using a food processor or blender, puree soup. Return soup to kettle and add milk. Gently heat and simmer 10 minutes, to give the flavors a chance to blend. Do not bring to a boil as milk will curdle.

Season to taste with salt and pepper. Garnish with pumpkin seeds.

Other vegetables can be substituted for zucchini. Potato can be substituted for rice.

SPLIT PEA SOUP

Serves 6-8

A homey soup to share with family and friends.

4 cups green split peas	**2 tablespoons dried parsley**
12 cups water or vegetable stock	**☐**
8 cloves garlic, minced	**1 teaspoon salt**
1 pound carrots, diced	**1 teaspoon black pepper**
a bay leaf	

Wash peas. Place them together with water, garlic, carrots, bay leaf and dried parsley in a soup kettle. Bring to a boil, reduce heat, cover, and simmer until split peas are tender, about 1-1/2 hours.

Season to taste with salt and pepper before serving.

SWEET CORN AND CHILE SOUP

Serves 6

A light corn soup from the Southwest with a hint of heat.

1 tablespoon olive oil
2 medium onions, chopped
4 cloves garlic, minced
□
3 cups corn kernels, fresh
    or frozen
2-1/2 cups water or vegetable
    broth
2 hot chile peppers, seeded
    and minced

2 cups milk or soy milk
2 medium zucchini, quartered
    lengthwise and
    sliced
2 tablespoons fresh lemon
    or lime juice
2 tomatoes, diced
2 tablespoons dried parsley

Gently warm olive oil in a large kettle. Saute onions and garlic. Stir in corn kernels, cover, and cook 4 minutes. Stir in water and chiles. Cover and simmer soup until corn is tender, about 15 minutes.

Using a slotted soup, scoop out 3/4 of corn mixture. Using a food processor or blender, puree. Return puree to soup kettle.

Add milk, zucchini, lemon juice, tomatoes, and parsley. Heat soup, but do not allow to come to a boil.

To serve, ladle into bowls and garnish with more parsley.

WINTRY VEGETABLE SOUP

Serves 10-12

The recipe for this thick, mild, wonderful soup was given to us by Barbara Wagner.

1/8 cup olive oil	1/2 pound carrots, diced
2 large onions, chopped	2 stalks celery, sliced
5 cloves garlic, minced	3 cups cooked garbanzo beans
□	4 cups cooked sweet potatoes, pureed
2 large potatoes, diced	1 teaspoon black pepper
1 cup dried lima beans	10 cups water or stock
1 pound corn kernels	salt to taste

Gently warm olive oil in a soup kettle. Saute onions and garlic until translucent.

Add remaining ingredients and bring soup to a boil. Cover pot, lower heat, and simmer until potatoes and lima beans are tender, about 45 minutes.

Salt to taste before serving.

YELLOW SQUASH AND SHRIMP BISQUE

Serves 6

Aromatic and delicious. Serve with crispy, brown bread and a tossed green salad.

1 large onion, chopped	**1/2 teaspoon thyme**
1 green pepper, chopped	**2 bay leaves**
1 pound yellow squash, sliced	**1 teaspoon salt**
1 large potato, diced	**2 tablespoons olive oil, optional**
5 cups water or vegetable stock	**□**
□	**1/2 pound medium raw shrimp,**
1/4 teaspoon cayenne pepper	**peeled and deveined**

Place onion, pepper, squash, and potato in a soup kettle with 2 cups water. Steam vegetables until potato can easily be pierced with a knife.

Using a food processor or blender, puree soup and return to kettle. Add remaining water and seasonings. Stir in olive oil, if desired.

Cut each shrimp into halves or thirds, depending on size. A piece of shrimp should easily fit onto a spoon. Add shrimp to soup and simmer 5 minutes. Shrimp will turn pink and flavor soup.

Taste and adjust seasoning.   Serve at once.

ZUCCHINI POTAGE

Serves 8

Tarragon, thyme, and dill enhance the flavor of this light-textured hot or cold soup.

1 large onion, quartered	1 teaspoon tarragon
3 large potatoes, unpeeled and diced	1/2 teaspoon thyme
	1 teaspoon black pepper
4 large zucchini, chunked	1/4 teaspoon cayenne pepper
5 cups water or stock	1 quart milk or soy milk
□	□
1 teaspoon dried dill	salt to taste
	fresh dill for garnish, optional

Steam onion, potatoes, and zucchini in a soup kettle with 5 cups water until potatoes can be easily pierced with a knife, about 10 minutes.

Using a food processor or blender, puree soup with just enough water from steaming vegetables so the mixture flows under the blades. Return soup and remaining vegetable stock to kettle. Add dill, tarragon, thyme, peppers and milk.

Stir soup over low heat until hot. Do not bring to a boil or milk will curdle. Turn flame off and let soup stand 10 minutes to give the flavors a chance to blend.

Taste and adjust seasoning. Serve hot or cold and garnish with snips of fresh dill.

Salads

Back at Kallimos . . .

"Today is the day the village makes soap," Hannah explained as we stared at the [village] green. . . .

. . . There were perhaps two dozen people standing and sitting right near the fire, mostly in groups of four or five. Others watched us from their porches. In all, there were seventy to eighty people on or around the green. They observed us closely but remained silent until Hannah began to speak in their language. Her words quickly melted their reserve. Smiles and friendly nods spread among them. Words of welcome, which we did not understand, followed quickly. Children, who had hidden behind their mothers, peeked out at us. . . .

continued . . .

. . . I asked Hannah how she had introduced us. She said, "I told the people that the rumors were true, that you two really were from the Other World, and I told them to welcome you. I also told them not to be afraid of you. I said, 'Do not fear the man's loud words, for inside he is a frightened boy. Your gentleness will soothe his troubled spirit.'"

With these simple words, we entered the world of Kallimos. Every member of the village came to our side. They smiled and laid their hands upon us. . . . Gradually, a circle formed around us. When the circle was complete, Hannah led a chant. The chant, which was repeated ten times, had a melody that I found very soothing. It was almost like a lullaby. According to Hannah, the chant in English would go as follows:

> *I give to you,*
> *From you I receive.*
> *Together we turn,*
> *And plant the seed.*

After the chant, the people of the village raised a loud, welcoming cheer that dissolved into laughter. With simple gestures and nods, they invited us to eat our first meal in their company. . . .

Excerpted from Learning from Hannah © *William H. Thomas, M.D.*

AVOCADO WITH CAULIFLOWER AND ROMAINE

Serves 6-8

Simply delicious! Remember: the fat in avocadoes is GOOD fat!

Salad

2 cups cauliflower florets
□

**1 head romaine, washed, torn
into bite-sized pieces,
and spun-dry in a salad
spinner**

**1 small red onion, halved and
cut into thin rings**

Dressing

1/4 cup olive oil
**1/4 cup cider or wine
vinegar**
1 teaspoon salt

1/2 teaspoon black pepper
**3 cloves garlic, mashed with
garlic press**

1 avocado

Steam cauliflower florets with 1 cup water until crisp-tender, about 5 minutes. Place in colander and rinse under cold water. Drain and place in salad bowl.

Add romaine and red onion. In a small bowl, whisk together dressing and pour over salad. Toss gently.

Peel and slice avocado. Serve salad using avocado as garnish.

BASIC TOSSED GREEN SALAD

Serves 4

Every tossed green salad we love has romaine lettuce as its base. The slightly bitter radicchio adds a rich, red color and the turnips add zing.

> **1 head romaine, washed and torn into bite-sized**
> **pieces, spun-dry in a salad spinner**
> **1 small head radicchio, torn into bite-sized pieces**
> **2 small carrots, grated**
> **1 small turnip, grated**
>
> **1/4-1/2 cup Debra's Olive Oil Vinaigrette (recipe on page 238)**

Place all the vegetables in a large salad bowl and pour dressing over. Toss gently until lettuce is well coated and carrots and turnips are dispersed.

Serve immediately.

Salad may also be simply dressed with balsamic vinegar, which keeps the calorie count low.

CABBAGE SALAD WITH SHRIMP AND WALNUTS

Serves 6

Cabbage is softened by shredding and an acidic dressing. Combined with walnuts, shrimp, and watercress, it becomes elegant!

4 tablespoons wine or cider vinegar
2 teaspoons Dijon-style mustard
1/4 cup olive oil
☐
1/2 medium head cabbage, cut into pieces to fit feed tube of a food processor, or sliced thinly by hand

4 whole scallions, sliced
1 bunch watercress, stemmed
☐
3/4 cup walnut halves or pieces
1/2 pound small cooked shrimp
1 teaspoon salt
1 teaspoon black pepper
☐
romaine leaves for each plate

Combine vinegar, mustard and olive oil in a salad bowl.

Slice cabbage using the thin slicing disk of a food processor and firm pressure, or slice by hand. Remove cabbage to bowl. Add scallions and watercress leaves and toss gently. Chill, covered, for one hour.

Meanwhile, toast walnuts on a cookie sheet in a 350 degree oven for 5 minutes. Remove from oven and cool completely.

Add walnuts, cooked shrimp, salt, and pepper to salad. Toss and serve.

For variety, substitute chicken or turkey for shrimp.

CAESAR SALAD

Serves 4

Garlic, anchovies, and Pecorino Romano. Heaven!

2-3 cloves garlic
1 teaspoon mustard powder
1 tablespoon lemon juice
3 tablespoons olive oil
a 3.5 oz. can anchovies
☐
**1/4 cup freshly grated Pecorino
   Romano cheese**

☐
**1 large head romaine lettuce,
   washed, broken into pieces
   and spun-dry in a salad
   spinner**
☐
**whole wheat croutons, optional
   (see recipe below)**

Crush garlic with a garlic press into a salad bowl. Add mustard, lemon and olive oil. Mash anchovies into dressing with a small fork until almost a paste.

Add romaine to the bowl. Toss until lettuce is well coated. Sprinkle salad with cheese and toss again. Add croutons if desired. Serve at once.

Croutons
   1/4 cup olive oil
   2 cups diced whole wheat bread (1/2" cubes)
   2 cloves garlic, mashed

Gently warm olive oil in skillet. Add bread and garlic. Saute over medium heat. Shake pan until croutons are browned.

Alternatively, mix bread with olive oil and garlic and place on cookie sheet in oven. Bake at 350 degrees until croutons are brown and crisp. Stir from time to time.

CUCUMBER YOGURT SALAD

Serves 4

A simple salad, which is a Middle-Eastern specialty.

1 clove garlic, mashed with garlic press	**1 English cucumber, or 4 pickling cukes**
1 teaspoon dried mint, or 3-4 fresh mint leaves, chopped	☐
1/4 teaspoon salt	**black pepper and salt to taste**
☐	**1 tablespoon olive oil**
2 cups low-fat plain yogurt	**1/4 cup raisins**
	1/4 cup chopped walnuts

Press garlic into a salad bowl. (If using fresh mint, mash well with garlic and salt before adding yogurt.) Add yogurt, blending completely.

Grate cucumbers with the shredding disk of a food processor. (Alternatively, you can halve cucumbers, then slice thinly.) Fold cucumbers into yogurt mixture together with olive oil, raisins, and walnuts.

Taste and add salt and pepper if desired.

This salad can be made without olive oil, raisins, or walnuts. It will still be refreshing and delicious! It also is wonderful with grated yellow squash and sliced radishes.

Serve at room temperature, or slightly chilled.

FRESH FRUIT SALAD

Serves 12

Vivid colors, a juxtaposition of sweet and tart, of shapes and textures. A feast for the eyes and tastebuds.

1 quart strawberries, washed, hulled, and halved	**2 cups blueberries**
2 cups fresh pineapple, peeled and chunked	**2 cups pitted bing cherries**
2 cups washed seedless green grapes	**4 kiwi, peeled and sliced**
6 peaches or nectarines, halved and sliced into wedges	**1 cup papaya or orange juice**
	few drops almond extract
	□
	2 bananas

Prepare fruit as directed above. Use a cherry pitter, a handy gadget, to plunge pits out of cherries.

Combine fruit, except bananas, with juice and a few drops of almond extract. Toss gently.

Cover and refrigerate for an hour to give the flavors a chance to blend.

Just before serving, slice in banana.

Fruit salad can be as simple as strawberries and grapes combined with a sliced banana or more elaborate than ours with the addition of mango, papaya, etc.

GLOWING SALAD

Serves 6

If you have a food processor, Glowing Salad takes 5 minutes to make. A wonderful cleansing salad, high in iron. Serve bedded on a leaf of romaine and garnish with a sprig of parsley or watercress and a slice of avocado.

2 medium carrots
3 medium apples, halved and
    cored
3 medium to large beets
    □
2 cups pineapple chunks in juice

1 teaspoon lemon juice
    □
parsley or watercress for
    garnish
romaine leaves, for bedding
slices of avocado, for garnish

Grate carrots, apples and beets with shredding disk of food processor. Alternatively, these vegetables can be grated by hand with an old-fashioned grater. Watch the knuckles though!

Place grated carrots, apples and beets in salad bowl and mix with pineapple, pineapple juice, and lemon. Toss until no clumps of apples remain. Add more pineapple juice if salad seems too dry.

Serve as suggested above.

GREEK ORZO SALAD WITH FETA AND SHRIMP

Serves 6

Orzo, a rice-shaped pasta, shrimp and salty feta combine the flavors of summer and the Mediterranean. An elegant picnic dish.

Dressing
- *1/4 cup fresh dill, minced, or*
  - *2 tablespoons dried dill weed*
- *2 cloves garlic, mashed*
- *3 tablespoons olive oil*
- *3 tablespoons lemon juice*
- *3 tablespoons cider vinegar*
- *1/2 teaspoon salt*
- *1 teaspoon black pepper*

Salad
- *1 pound medium shrimp, peeled, deveined, and steamed until pink*
  - ☐
- *1 pound orzo, cooked, rinsed, drained and tossed with 1 tablespoon olive oil*
- *1/2 cup feta cheese, crumbled*
- *1 large ripe tomato, diced*
- *1/2 cup pitted, Greek-style, garlic or jalapeno-stuffed olives, sliced*
- *1 bunch flat Italian parsley, chopped*
- *1 small bunch scallions, sliced*
  - ☐
- *romaine lettuce leaves and sprigs of dill for garnish*

Combine dressing ingredients in a large bowl. Add steamed shrimp and toss.

To cook orzo: bring water to a boil in a large pot. Add pasta and cook until tooth-tender, about 7 minutes. Remove pasta to mesh colander and rinse with cold water.

To the bowl, add the cooked orzo, crumbled feta, tomato, olives, parsley, and scallions. Toss gently and adjust seasoning.

Serve salad bedded on a romaine lettuce leaf and garnished with a sprig of fresh dill.

GREEK SHRIMP AND POTATO SALAD A LA PAPPAS

Serves 8

Sunday afternoons, growing up in Florida, we used to drive to Tarpon Springs to order Pappas potato salad. Here's a fond memory of this wholemeal feast.

8 large white potatoes, boiled
□
8 sprigs fresh parsley, chopped
4 whole scallions, sliced
1 green bell pepper, chopped
1/4 cup olive oil
2 tablespoons wine vinegar
2 cloves garlic, mashed with
  garlic press
1 teaspoon salt
□
1 head romaine, washed, torn into
  bite-sized pieces
□
12 sprigs watercress
1 unwaxed cucumber, sliced
1 avocado, peeled, pitted and
  sliced

1/4 pound feta cheese, sliced
4 large shrimp per person,
  peeled, deveined and
  steamed 4 minutes
a 3.5-oz can anchovy fillets
12 Greek olives
1 radish per person
1 whole scallion per person
1 ripe tomato per person,
  cut into wedges
□
1 tablespoon olive oil
  per person
1 tablespoon wine vinegar
  per person
dried oregano

Drain boiled potatoes. When cool enough to handle, peel and slice. While still warm, toss with parsley, scallions, green pepper, olive oil, vinegar, garlic and salt.

Bed 8 dinner plates with romaine. Divide potato salad by mounding spoonfuls in the center of each plate.

continued . . .

GREEK SHRIMP AND POTATO SALAD A LA PAPPAS
(continued)

Decoratively arrange sprigs of watercress, sliced cucumber, sliced avocado, feta cheese, four jumbo shrimp per person, and anchovy fillets on each plate. Place a radish in the center and a scallion and a wedge of tomato to one side.

Drizzle 1 tablespoon olive oil and 1 tablespoon wine vinegar over each plate. Sprinkle with oregano.

Serve at once. Be mindful that these portions are large. The only thing that should follow this meal is fresh fruit. A bowl of berries would be nice.

ISRAELI SALAD

Serves 6

Our rendition of salad eaten in Israel for breakfast or dinner. Accompany with thick slices of dark bread and soft white cheese.

6 large, ripe tomatoes cut into bite-size pieces
1 English cucumber, quartered lengthwise and sliced, or 4 pickling cukes, diced
2 red or green bell peppers, diced
1 red or white sweet onion, minced

1 yellow squash, diced
4 tablespoons parsley, minced
4 tablespoons fresh lemon juice
4 tablespoons olive oil
2 cloves garlic, minced or mashed with garlic press
1 teaspoon black pepper
1 teaspoon salt

Prepare and place the vegetables in a salad bowl.

Add the lemon juice, olive oil, garlic, pepper and salt to salad. Mix gently and serve.

MARINATED MUSHROOM SALAD

Serves 8

A la Grecque. Subtle flavors and contrasting textures.

1 pound mushrooms, thickly sliced	2 cloves garlic, mashed with a garlic press, or
1 red bell pepper, quartered lengthwise and sliced thinly	1/2 teaspoon garlic powder
	1 teaspoon paprika
4 small zucchini, sliced	1/2 teaspoon oregano
4 whole scallions, sliced	1/2 teaspoon basil
1/4 cup olive oil	1/2 teaspoon thyme
1/4 cup cider vinegar	1/2 teaspoon rosemary

Prepare vegetables and place in salad bowl.

In a small bowl, whisk together oil, vinegar, herbs and spices. Pour over vegetables and toss gently.

Refrigerate salad, covered, for several hours. Toss again, taste, and adjust seasoning. Add salt if desired.

Makes a wonderful addition to an antipasto.

NO-OIL DELI SALAD

Serves 6

Cool, crunchy, and multi-colored. Deli Salad tastes like pickles after the first day!

1 large English cucumber, or
   3 small pickling cukes, cut in
   half lengthwise and sliced
   1/4" thick
2-3 thinly sliced carrots
2 sweet red or yellow bell
   peppers, diced in large
   pieces

1 sweet red onion, minced
1 yellow squash, diced
1 kohlrabi, peeled and diced
   □
1/2 cup cider vinegar
1/2 cup water
black pepper to taste

Combine vegetables in a shallow glass or stainless steel bowl or container. Pour vinegar and water over the vegetables, cover and marinate in the refrigerator for an hour, or longer.

Stir salad every so often if vegetables are not covered by marinade.

Fun to take on picnics. Does not wilt and requires no salt.

PEPPERY SLAW

Serves 6-8

Our favorite coleslaw. Entertaining is easy because this is prepared 24-48 hours in advance.

2 pounds green cabbage, cut into chunks to fit the feed tube of a food processor
8 red radishes, sliced
1 medium sweet red onion, sliced thinly
1 kohlrabi, peeled and grated
2 carrots, grated
❑

5 sprigs fresh dill or 1 tablespoon dill seeds
❑
1/4 cup olive oil
1/3 cup cider vinegar
1 teaspoon black pepper
1/2 teaspoon white pepper
1/2 teaspoon cayenne pepper
salt, if desired, to taste

Using the slicing disk of a food processor, slice cabbage, radishes and onion with firm pressure. Alternatively, slice thinly by hand. Place vegetables in a salad bowl. Insert grating disk and grate kohlrabi and carrots. Add to salad bowl.

Snip fresh dill into salad using scissors, or add dill seeds.

Whisk together olive oil, vinegar, black pepper, white pepper, and cayenne pepper. Pour dressing over slaw and toss, mixing thoroughly. Cover and refrigerate. Before serving, stir, taste, and adjust seasonings.

POTATO SALAD WITH OLIVE OIL AND OREGANO

Serves 8

Don't stint on the olive oil - it won't be the same! Best served warm. After you taste this, you'll wonder how you ever liked potato salad with mayonnaise.

**6 large white potatoes, quartered
  and steamed in their jackets,
  or 10 cups little red
  potatoes, steamed in
  their jackets**
  ☐
**1 large sweet white or red onion,
  minced**

4 stalks celery, sliced
**4 hard-boiled eggs, peeled
  and sliced**
1 cup fresh or frozen peas
1 tablespoon dried oregano
1 teaspoon salt
1 teaspoon black pepper
1/2 cup olive oil

When potatoes are cool enough to handle, cut into bite-sized pieces and put in salad bowl.

Add onions, celery, eggs, peas, oregano, salt, pepper and olive oil. Toss gently.

Delicious when served warm.

RICE PASTA WITH BOK CHOY AND CASHEWS

Serves 8

Rice pasta combines with bolder flavors and the richness of ground cashews. A salad which keeps well.

10 ounce box Pastariso rice spaghetti, or other rice pasta

Dressing

4 tablespoon sesame oil
4 tablespoons tamari sauce
1/2 teaspoon fennel seed
1/2 teaspoon dried basil

1/4 teaspoon cayenne pepper
3 cloves garlic, minced
1/2 teaspoon cumin
1 teaspoon black pepper, optional

Salad

3 stalks celery, sliced diagonally into strips
7 stalks bok choy, julienned
bok choy leaves shredded
1 5-oz. can sliced water chestnuts

1 bunch scallions, sliced
1 cup roasted cashews, coarsely chopped
☐
salt to taste, if desired

Cook spaghetti according to directions on the box. Meanwhile, prepare dressing and place in salad bowl. When pasta is al dente, pour into colander and run under cold water. Shake off as much water as possible and place pasta in bowl with dressing, gently separating and coating strands as you mix.

Add celery and bok choy. Cut scallion bottoms in half lengthwise, then slice. Add to salad together with water chestnuts and cashews. Toss salad until all ingredients are evenly dispersed. Taste, adjust seasoning and serve at room temperature.

SALAD WITH WATERCRESS, RADICCHIO AND PINE NUTS

Serves 6

A tossed, green salad accented with buttery, sweet pine nuts.

Salad

*1 cup green beans, cut into
2-inch pieces*
☐
*1 small red onion, halved and cut
into thin rings*
1 bunch watercress, stemmed

*1 head radicchio, torn into
bite-sized pieces, washed
and spun dry*
*1 head romaine, torn into
bite-sized pieces, washed
and spun dry*
1/2 cup pine nuts

Dressing

*3 tablespoons cider or
wine vinegar*
1/4 cup olive oil
1 teaspoon salt
1/2 teaspoon mustard powder
1/2 teaspoon black pepper

*4 cloves garlic mashed in
a garlic press*
1 teaspoon oregano
1/2 teaspoon thyme
1/2 teaspoon basil

Steam string beans in several tablespoons of water until crisp-tender, about 3 minutes. Place in colander and rinse with cold water. Drain and place in salad bowl.

Add remaining vegetables and pine nuts to bowl.

Whisk together dressing and pour over salad. Toss gently until romaine and radicchio are well coated. Taste, adjust seasoning, and serve immediately.

SPINACH-CARROT SALAD WITH YOGURT DRESSING

Serves 4

No oil in this dressing. If you don't tell, they won't notice.

Salad
  - 1 pound fresh spinach
  - 4 carrots, grated
  - 1 small white onion, halved and cut into thin rings

Dressing
  - 1 cup low or no-fat yogurt
  - 1 teaspoon salt
  - 2 teaspoons lemon juice
  - 3 cloves garlic, mashed with a garlic press
  - 1/4 teaspoon oregano
  - 1/4 teaspoon marjoram
  - 1/2 teaspoon black pepper

  - 1 hard-boiled egg, chopped, optional

Wash spinach, trim stems, and tear into bite-sized pieces. Spin dry in a salad spinner. Place in a salad bowl together with grated carrots and onion rings.

In a small bowl, whisk together dressing and pour over salad. Toss until spinach and carrots are well coated.

Garnish with chopped egg and serve immediately.

The tartness of this dressing complements the sweetness of carrots. A teaspoon of honey may be added if the salad is too tart for your taste.

SPINACH-LETTUCE SALAD WITH CHOPPED EGG

Serves 4-6

A vibrant, dressed-up version of an old favorite. Dark green, brilliant red, yellow, and white. A colorful taste to match.

1 pound fresh spinach	1/4 cup olive oil
1 head Boston lettuce	1 tablespoon cider vinegar
1 small head radicchio	or lemon juice
☐	1/2 teaspoon salt
1 red onion, quartered and	1 teaspoon black pepper
thinly sliced	☐
☐	1 hard-boiled egg
2 cloves garlic, mashed with	nasturtium flowers for garnish,
garlic press	optional

Wash spinach, lettuce and radicchio and tear into bite-sized pieces. Spin dry in salad spinner. Place in a salad bowl together with onions.

In a small bowl, whisk together garlic, olive oil, vinegar, salt and pepper and pour over salad. Toss until greens are coated.

Add diced egg to salad. When in season, add nasturtium flowers to add more color and spice. Serve immediately.

THAI TURKEY SALAD

Serves 9

An adaptation of a Thai dish, which is spicy and light. Best eaten the day it's made so the bean sprouts are still crunchy.

2 pounds turkey thigh or breast
□
4 tablespoons lemon juice
2 tablespoons tamari sauce
3 jalapeno peppers, seeded
  and minced
4 cloves garlic, minced
1 small red onion, thinly sliced
1 teaspoon dried basil

2 cups mung bean sprouts
2 cups shredded Chinese
  cabbage
1 small bunch radishes, halved
  and sliced
□
black pepper to taste

Poach turkey in simmering water for about an hour, until juices run clear when turkey is pierced with a knife. Remove turkey from liquid and let cool.

Discard skin, remove meat from bones and shred (fingers work fine). There should be about 2 cups turkey meat.

While turkey simmers, stir together lemon juice, tamari, peppers, garlic, red onion and basil. Place in salad bowl, cover and let mixture marinate at room temperature until needed.

Together with remaining ingredients, add turkey to bowl. Toss well. Add pepper to taste.

TOFU ANTIPASTO SALAD

Serves 12

Cool, refreshing, and a great way to fall in love with tofu. This salad keeps well for 2-3 days.

10 ounces mushrooms, sliced thickly
4 stalks celery, sliced
2 cups fresh or canned tomato chunks
2 sweet green bell peppers, diced
1 bunch Italian flat parsley, chopped

1 package firm or extra-firm tofu, chunked
1/2 cup pitted olives, chopped coarsely
□
2 tablespoons olive oil
1/3 cup lemon juice
1 teaspoon oregano
salt and pepper to taste

Prepare vegetables and olives and place in salad bowl together with tofu. Add remaining ingredients and toss gently to mix. Taste and add salt and pepper if desired.

Marinate antipasto at room temperature for 30 minutes. May be prepared 24 hours ahead and stored overnight in the refrigerator.

TONGOL TUNA SALAD

Serves 6

Tuna salad on the lighter side.

Three 6.5 ounce cans no-salt Tongol Tuna
1 red bell pepper, diced
1 sweet green bell pepper, diced
1/2 medium red onion, diced
2 stalks celery, sliced

1/4 cup yogurt
1/4 cup mayonnaise or Nayonnaise*
1 tablespoon lemon juice
1 teaspoon black pepper

Place all ingredients in a salad bowl. Mix with a rubber spatula, but leave tuna in fairly large pieces. Do not mash or make tuna too smooth!

*Nayonnaise is a soy bean mayonnaise which contains no cholesterol. It can be found in any natural food store.

Bean and Grain Salads

Back at Kallimos . . .

Hannah's home, like ours, is a one-story cottage with an inviting front porch and one sparsely furnished room. In the fashion of all the homes here, the walls are thick, and vegetation hangs around the place like a fragrant, living curtain.

Jude and I tingled with excitement as we made our way there. We stepped onto the porch, knocked on her door, and were greeted with a smile as Hannah swung the door open. The scent of flowers and spices billowed out from the cottage. Hannah invited us to sit down on the benches that surrounded the fire pit. Our timing was perfect, she said, because she had just started to prepare our meal. According to Hannah, the people of Kallimos regard the preparation of a meal to be part of the meal itself. We talked casually as she conjured a feast of spicy roast peppers and rice from her simple provisions. I have never eaten better food. Our dessert was a small bottle of sweet, fruity wine.

Excerpted from Learning from Hannah © *William H. Thomas, M.D.*

ANTIPASTO CANNELLINI BEAN SALAD

Serves 8

4 cups cooked cannellini (white
    kidney) beans
2 cloves garlic, mashed in garlic
    press, or 1/2 teaspoon garlic
    powder
1/4 teaspoon thyme
1 teaspoon black pepper
8 fresh plum tomatoes, chopped
    coarsely
2 small red onions, minced
4 small celery ribs with leaves,
    sliced
1 bunch scallions, sliced

1 teaspoon dried, or
    2 tablespoons fresh basil
    (shredded)
several sprigs flat Italian
    parsley, chopped
1/4 cup olive oil
1/4 cup wine vinegar or
    lemon juice
    ☐
salt, if desired, to taste
extra tomatoes for garnish
olives for garnish, optional

Place cooked, cooled beans in salad bowl. Add remaining ingredients and toss gently to mix. Taste and adjust seasoning.

Cover salad and let stand at room temperature for an hour to give flavors the chance to blend. (Salad can be prepared a day in advance up to this point and refrigerated, covered.)

Serve at room temperature with wedges of juicy, ripe red tomatoes and olives.

APPLE PEANUT CURRY SALAD

Serves 8

Contrasting tastes and textures. Serve on a bed of red and green leaf lettuce.

Dressing
1 quart plain low or no-fat yogurt	*2 tablespoons lemon juice*
1 teaspoon curry powder	*pinch cayenne pepper*

Salad
6 large tart apples (Granny Smiths are great), wedged with apple slicer	*1 small red onion, diced, optional*
	1 cup roasted peanuts
1 cup cooked chickpeas, drained	*1 cup date pieces in oat flour*

Make dressing and place in salad bowl. Cut apples into wedges. If apples are large and a wedge won't fit comfortably into the mouth, cut again in half. Place apples in bowl and coat with dressing to prevent browning. Add remaining ingredients. Mix, chill for an hour and serve.

Best served the day it's made so the apples are nice and crisp. Curry intensifies and yogurt thickens as the salad stands.

BLACK BEAN JALAPENO SALAD

Serves 8

Black Bean Jalapeno Salad makes a dramatic presentation and can be tossed together at the last minute if one has cooked or canned black beans.

A colorful addition to a buffet or picnic spread. Black Bean Jalapeno Salad travels well and disappears quickly!

4 cups cooked black beans (or 2-16 ounce cans, rinsed and drained)	**1/2 teaspoon coriander**
	2 tablespoons corn oil
2 red bell peppers, diced	**2 tablespoons lime juice**
1 yellow bell pepper, diced	**1/2 teaspoon salt**
2 green bell peppers, diced	**1/4 teaspoon black**
1 bunch scallions, sliced	**pepper**
2 jalapeno peppers, seeded and minced	**pinch cayenne**

Place black beans in a bowl. (If beans are still hot, place in a colander and run under cold water to cool.)

Add sweet bell peppers, scallions, jalapeno pepper, coriander, oil, lime juice, salt and pepper and toss until beans are well coated.

If a spicier version is desired, leave in a few jalapeno seeds, or add more cayenne.

DILLED VEGETABLES WITH MILLET

Serves 6-8

Millet, a mild, wonderful grain, is also easy to digest.   For a different effect, crumble bleu cheese over the salad.

Salad

1 cup millet	2 cups string beans, cut into
2 cups water	2" pieces
☐	2 small zucchini, halved
2 cups cauliflower florets	and sliced thinly
2 cups broccoli florets	1 small red onion, minced

Dressing

1/3 cup olive oil	1/4 teaspoon basil
3 tablespoons cider vinegar	1/4 teaspoon tarragon
3 tablespoons lemon juice	1 teaspoon black pepper
1 tablespoon fresh dill, or	2 cloves garlic, mashed with
1 teaspoon dried dill weed	garlic press
1 teaspoon salt	1 cup bleu cheese, optional

To cook millet, bring water to a boil, stir in grain, cover, and simmer 40 minutes. Turn heat off and leave cover on pot for ten minutes more.   Place millet in bowl and fluff with fork occasionally until cool.

Steam cauliflower and broccoli with 1 cup water for about 5 minutes, or until crisp-tender. Place vegetables in a colander, rinse under cold water, and drain.   Add to salad bowl. Steam string beans with 1/2 cup water for 3 minutes. Cool under running water, drain, and add to salad together with zucchini and onion.

In a small bowl, whisk dressing. Pour over salad. Toss gently. Crumble in blue cheese if desired. Cover and refrigerate for an hour before serving.

FAGIOLIO (HARICOT BEANS) WITH CHICKEN

Serves 4

Fagiolio with chicken makes a light meal with crusty brown bread warm from the oven, or is a wonderful addition to a colorful antipasto.

Salad
- **2 cups cooked haricot beans**
- **1 cup cooked, boned chicken, shredded**
- **1 bunch watercress, stemmed**
- **1 medium white onion, minced**
   □
- **1/2 medium head cabbage, finely shredded**

Dressing
- **4 tablespoons olive oil**
- **4 tablespoons lemon juice**
- **1 tablespoon dried basil**
- **1/2 teaspoon salt**
- **1 teaspoon black pepper**
   □
- **black olives for garnish, optional**

Place haricot beans, chicken, watercress leaves and minced onion into a serving bowl.

Cut cabbage in chunks to fit feed tube of a food processor and finely shred using the slicing disk. Add cabbage to salad. Alternatively, slice finely by hand.

Whisk together dressing ingredients. Pour over salad and toss until mixed. Taste and adjust seasoning. Serve garnished with black olives.

LENTIL BULGUR SALAD WITH FETA CHEESE

Serves 8-10

One of our favorites. Best eaten at room temperature, so it's a great picnic salad, or one to make when you're having company and the refrigerator is full.

	Dressing
1-1/2 cups boiling water	
1-1/2 cups bulgur	**2/3 cup olive oil**
☐	**2/3 cup cider vinegar**
1-1/2 cups lentils	**1 tablespoon dried basil, or**
5 cups water	**3 tablespoons fresh**
☐	**2 tablespoons dill seed**
2 bunches whole scallions, sliced	**1 teaspoon salt**
1 large bunch Italian flat parsley,	**1 teaspoon black pepper**
chopped	☐
1 green bell pepper, diced	**1-1/2 cups feta cheese**
1 red bell pepper, diced	

Pour boiling water over bulgur and let stand until liquid is absorbed, about 30 minutes. Meanwhile bring 5 cups water to a boil, add washed lentils, and simmer until tender, about 20 minutes. Do not overcook or they turn to mush. Drain lentils and transfer to serving bowl with the bulgur.

Fluff grains and lentils with a fork every once in awhile until cool. Meanwhile, prepare vegetables.

Once grain and lentils are cool, add vegetables. Pour dressing over salad. Toss with a rubber spatula to mix well. Crumble in feta and toss again. Let salad stand, covered, for several hours before serving.

MOROCCAN COUSCOUS

Serves 10

Slightly sweet and very colorful. A favorite with children.

Salad

2 cups couscous	2 red bell peppers,
2 cups boiling water	diced
☐	2 cups peas
1 cup pine nuts, dry roasted	1 small red onion, minced
☐	1 bunch Italian flat parsley,
4 carrots, halved and diced	chopped
2 cups green beans, cut into	1 cup raisins
2" pieces	

Dressing

2 tablespoons olive oil	1 cup apple juice
2 tablespoons lemon juice	pinch cayenne
1 teaspoon salt	pinch black pepper

Place couscous in a bowl. Pour over boiling water and let stand 15 minutes for grain to absorb water. Fluff with fork occasionally to cool and break apart clumps of grain.

Toast pine nuts by stirring in a skillet over medium heat until golden, about 3 minutes. Cool.

Steam carrots in 1 cup water for five minutes, until crisp-tender. Steam beans in 1/2 cup water 3 minutes. Place vegetables in colander, rinse under cold water, drain, and add to couscous. Stir in peppers, peas, red onion, parsley and raisins.

In a small bowl, whisk dressing and pour over salad. Add pine nuts and toss. Let stand an hour for the flavors to blend.

PEA, ARTICHOKE HEART AND CHEDDAR

Serves 12

Pour dressing on warm chickpeas, because they, like potatoes, are more absorbent when warm. This salad is a meal in itself.

Dressing

2 tablespoons olive oil
2 tablespoons lemon juice or
  cider vinegar
2 cloves garlic, mashed with
  a garlic press

1 teaspoon salt
1 teaspoon black pepper
1/2 teaspoon oregano

Salad

3 cups cooked, still warm
  chickpeas
2 cups raw or frozen peas
3/4 pound cheddar, cubed
1 14-ounce can artichoke hearts
  in water, quartered

1 bunch Italian flat parsley,
  chopped coarsely
1 red or yellow pepper,
  diced

Whisk dressing together.

Place chickpeas, peas, cheddar, artichoke hearts, chopped parsley, and red pepper in a salad bowl. Pour over dressing and toss until chickpeas are coated.

Allow salad to marinate for 30 minutes to an hour at room temperature.

Serve at room temperature.

QUINOA WITH PINE NUTS AND APRICOTS

Serves 4

Quinoa, an ancient grain rediscovered, is a complete protein. It also sprouts as it cooks. Because the Indians believed quinoa gave them superhuman powers, Cortez made having it or eating it punishable by death.

2 cups water	**1/2 teaspoon ground coriander**
1 cup quinoa	**2 tablespoons olive oil**
☐	**1/4 cup dried apricots,**
1/2 cup toasted pine nuts	**chopped coarsely**
☐	**1 bunch scallions, thinly sliced**
1 teaspoon salt	**1 red bell pepper finely**
1 tablespoon fresh lemon juice	**diced, or 3 tablespoons**
1 teaspoon paprika	**dried sweet bell peppers**
1 teaspoon ground cumin	

In a medium saucepan, bring water to a boil. Stir in quinoa, cover pot, and simmer for 10 minutes. Turn off flame and let quinoa remain in the covered pot for another 10 minutes so grain will absorb water.

Transfer quinoa to a salad bowl and fluff slightly with a fork every few minutes until grain cools.

Toast pine nuts in a dry skillet over moderate heat, stirring until nuts are golden brown, about 3 minutes. Set aside.

When the quinoa is cool, add remaining ingredients and toss until grain is coated. Serve and enjoy.

RED AND WILD RICE SALAD

Serves 8

Wild rice with its earthy aroma, chewy wehani or Thai red rice, and toasted sunflower seeds make an interesting combination. Garnish with marigold flowers in summer.

2 cups wehani or Thai red rice	**1 bunch scallions, sliced**
1 cup wild rice	**1 teaspoon oregano**
6 cups water	☐
☐	**1/4 cup olive oil**
2 cups sunflower seeds	**1/4 cup lemon juice**
1 bunch flat Italian parsley,	** or 1/2 teaspoon salt**
** chopped**	**1 teaspoon black pepper**
	1/4 teaspoon cayenne pepper

Bring water to a boil. Stir in rice, cover pot, lower heat and simmer 45 minutes. When rice is cooked, let sit in pot with the cover on for another 10 minutes to absorb moisture.

Place rice in a bowl. Fluff with a fork from time to time until cool.

Dry-toast sunflower seeds by stirring in a skillet until seeds begin to brown - be careful not to burn!

Once rice is cool, add remaining ingredients. Mix well. If desired, garnish with marigold flowers, which have a slightly bitter flavor.

Best served warm or at room temperature.

RED-LEAF LETTUCE GARBANZO SALAD

Serves 6

An easy and informal dinner salad. Serve with sourdough bread or whole wheat dinner rolls. Honeydew and cantaloupe slices make a grand finale.

Salad

1 cup cooked garbanzo beans
  □
2 small yellow squash, thinly sliced
1 bunch scallions, sliced
2 small carrots, grated
1 head red leaf lettuce, washed, torn into bite-sized pieces and spun dry

1/2 pound spinach, torn into bite-sized pieces, washed, and spun dry
1 cup peas
1/2 pound cheddar or Monterey Jack cheese or soy cheese, cubed

Dressing

1/3 cup olive oil
1/3 cup cider vinegar
4 cloves garlic mashed in a garlic press

pinch each oregano, basil, and marjoram
1/2 teaspoon salt
1 teaspoon black pepper

Place warm garbanzo beans in a salad bowl.

In a small bowl, whisk dressing together and pour over beans.

Prepare vegetables as directed above and add, together with cheese, to salad. Toss gently until lettuce and spinach leaves are well coated and cheese is evenly distributed.

Serve immediately.

RYE BERRY AND BARLEY SALAD

Serves 4-6

Mild, chewy grains combine with colorful vegetables and a zingy dressing. A great summer salad that keeps well.

1/2 cup uncooked rye berries
1/2 cup uncooked barley
3 cups water
□
1 pound carrots, diced
□
1 bunch scallions, sliced
1/2 red bell pepper, diced
1/2 green bell pepper, diced
1/2 orange or yellow bell
   pepper, diced

1 bunch parsley, chopped
□
1 tablespoon olive oil
2 tablespoons cider vinegar
2 tablespoons lemon juice
1-2 teaspoons dried dill weed
1 teaspoon black pepper
1 teaspoon salt
pinch cayenne pepper

Place rye berries and barley in a large pot together with water. Bring to a boil, lower heat, cover, and simmer for about 1-1/4 hours, until water is absorbed and grains are tender.

Place grains in a colander and run cold water over to cool. Shake colander to allow as much water as possible to drain.

While rye and barley are cooking, prepare remaining vegetables. Steam carrots for 3-4 minutes in 2 cups water, or until crisp-tender. Cool under running water. Drain and place in a salad bowl. Add remaining vegetables. When ready, spoon in grains, and pour over dressing and mix well.

As with all grain and bean salads, this is best served at room temperature.

SOUTHWESTERN SALAD

Serves 8

A vibrant, crunchy salad with the spicy-sweet flavors of the Southwest. Although it can be served cold, we prefer it room temperature.

2 cups cooked kidney, pinto, or navy beans
2 jalapeno peppers, seeded and finely minced
2 red bell peppers, diced
2 green bell peppers, diced
2 cups corn kernels, fresh or frozen
1 tablespoon cumin

2 teaspoons black pepper
pinch cayenne pepper
1/4 cup cider vinegar
2 tablespoons olive oil
1/2 teaspoon salt
□
18 cherry tomatoes, cut in half as garnish
1 bunch scallions, thinly sliced

Combine beans, sweet peppers, jalapeno peppers, corn, cumin, pepper, vinegar, olive oil, and salt. Toss until beans are well coated.

Add tomatoes and scallions, and gently toss salad again. Taste, adjust seasoning, and serve.

SPINACH, ZUCCHINI AND FETA

Serves 12

Irresistible and spirited. When zucchini flowers abound in the summer garden, use to garnish.

2 cups uncooked lentils
4 cups water
1 pound raw spinach
2 cups raw or frozen peas
4 medium zucchini, halved
  and thinly sliced
1 bunch scallions, sliced, or 1
  small red onion, minced
  □
1/3 cup olive oil
1/3 cup lemon or cider vinegar

2 garlic cloves, crushed or
  finely chopped
  □
1 cup crumbled feta cheese
1 teaspoon black pepper
salt to taste
  □
zucchini flowers for garnish,
  optional
lemon wedges for garnish,
  optional

Bring water to a boil. Add lentils, cover, lower heat, and cook for 20 minutes, until just tooth-tender. Do not overcook. Pour lentils into mesh colander or strainer. Run under cold water and shake gently to drain as much water as possible.

Coarsely chop spinach. Place spinach, lentils, peas, zucchini and scallions in a salad bowl.

Whisk together oil, lemon or vinegar, and garlic. Pour over ingredients in salad bowl. Crumble feta cheese into bowl with hands, add pepper, and toss salad gently. Taste and add salt if desired. Serve garnished with zucchini flowers or lemon wedges.

TABOULI

Serves 6

In the Middle East, tabouli is wrapped inside lettuce leaves and eaten with the fingers, or served inside pita with tahini sauce.

1-1/4 cups bulgur or cracked wheat	**1 cup cooked garbanzo beans**
1-1/4 cups boiling water	**1/4 cup lemon juice**
☐	**1/8 cup olive oil**
1 bunch parsley, minced	**1/2 teaspoon salt**
4 whole scallions, sliced	**1 teaspoon black pepper**
	1 cup diced tomato

Place bulgur in a large bowl and pour over boiling water. Let stand until water is absorbed, about 30 minutes. Then fluff grain with fork from time to time.

When bulgur is cool, add parsley, scallions, cooked garbanzo beans, lemon juice, olive oil, salt, pepper and diced tomato. Toss thoroughly. Let stand, covered, for an hour to give the flavors a chance to blend.

Serve on a bed of romaine lettuce.

Rather than mixing tomato into the tabouli, one can serve slices of tomato on the side as a garnish.

ZUCCHINI WHITE BEAN SALAD

Serves 10

Serve as part of an antipasto with roasted peppers, cheese and a loaf of whole grain French bread, or as a light meal with fresh berries and peaches for dessert.

Salad
- **4 zucchini, thinly sliced**
- **2 carrots, thinly sliced**
- **1 bunch scallions, sliced**
- **1 small red onion, minced**
- **1 cup cooked white beans**
- **1 bunch watercress, stemmed**

Dressing
- **3 tablespoons olive oil**
- **1/4 cup cider vinegar**
- **1/2 teaspoon tarragon**

- **2 cloves garlic, mashed with garlic press, or 1/2 teaspoon garlic powder**
- **1/2 teaspoon dry mustard powder**
- **1/2 teaspoon salt**
- **1 teaspoon black pepper**
- ☐ **Greek olives, optional for garnish**

Combine salad ingredients in a bowl. Whisk dressing ingredients together and pour over salad. Toss to mix thoroughly, making sure zucchini slices are separated.

Let salad stand, covered, in the refrigerator for several hours or overnight.

To serve, taste, adjust seasoning, and garnish with olives. Serve at room temperature.

Pasta and Cheese Main Dishes

Back at Kallimos . . .

"Tell me," said Hannah, "why do elders exist?"

This was a new question for us. We had always taken the presence of older adults for granted.

"All living things decline with advancing age," I said uncertainly, trying to feel my way toward an answer. "People are born, they mature, and they get old. That's the way life is."

"The living creatures of this world get older everyday, that's true enough," Hannah replied. "But in the long history of this good Earth, only human beings have protected their elderly from harm. For all other creatures, death follows hard on the heels of decline." . . .

"I see what you mean," Jude said thoughtfully. "There is a difference between becoming old and becoming elderly. Becoming old is a universal reality of biology; becoming elderly requires protection by others."

continued . . .

I picked up where Jude left off. "Do you realize what you are saying, Hannah? By your standard, an elder is one who relies on the support and protection of the village for survival. Thus, an elder, by definition, is a burden on the community. Is this any way to think of the elderly? Who could ever look forward to becoming a burden on their community?"

Hannah chose her words carefully. "You think only of what the village bestows upon the elder. . . ."

Hannah smiled gently, "Elders exist because they teach us how to make a community. As we give to them, they give to us their wisdom, their experience, their affection. When we come together to meet their needs, we learn how to live as human beings. They instruct us in the art of caring. There is no more precious a gift than that. The best communities are those most willing to pick up and carry the burdens of their frailest elders."

Jude leaned back and breathed a deep sigh. "So that's it," she said. "That's why this place feels so different from home. This village has wrapped itself around its elders. Serving them has given you gentleness and patience."

Adapted from Learning from Hannah © *William H. Thomas, M.D.*

ANCHOVY PUTTANESCA WITH PASTA

Serves 6

A mildly spicy sauce, which tastes wonderful hot or cold.

grated Pecorino Romano, optional ☐	2 sprigs fresh basil, minced
	1/2 teaspoon marjoram
2 tablespoons olive oil	1 teaspoon oregano
3 cloves garlic ☐	3 teaspoons dried hot pepper flakes
3.5-ounce can anchovy fillets ☐	black pepper, to taste ☐
4 cups tomato puree	1-1/2 pounds spaghetti

Gently warm olive oil in a skillet. Crush garlic with a garlic press and saute in oil until golden. Add anchovy fillets and mash with a fork. Add tomato puree, basil, marjoram, oregano and pepper to skillet. Simmer sauce 15 minutes, stirring occasionally, until quite flavorful and thickened.

While sauce is simmering, bring 4 quarts water to a rollicking boil. Add spaghetti and stir gently. When pasta is al dente, firm to the tooth, about 7 minutes, drain and place in a large bowl. Spoon sauce over pasta and mix gently until well coated.

Serve immediately and pass the grated cheese.

CALZONES WITH CHEESE AND PESTO

Serves 6   *Bake at 450*

Too delicious for words! There are many variations of calzones. Look for another one in the poultry chapter.

Dough
>   **1-1/2 teaspoons baking yeast**   **1/4 cup olive oil**
>   **1 cup lukewarm water**   **☐**
>   **1 teaspoon honey**   **3 cups whole wheat flour**
>   **1 teaspoon salt**

Sprinkle yeast over warm water and honey. Stir to dissolve. Let mixture stand 5 minutes, or until yeast is foamy. Stir in olive oil.

Whirl flour and salt together using the steel blade of a food processor. With machine running, add yeast mixture through the feed tube.

Process until dough is smooth and cleans the sides of the workbowl, about 30 seconds. Add a little more water (a teaspoonful at a time) if dough will not form a ball, or a bit more flour if dough seems sticky. (Dough will be somewhat sticky until after first rise.) Knead 15-20 seconds. Place dough in bowl. Cover with plastic wrap or a shower cap and let rise until doubled in bulk, about 30 minutes.

continued . . .

CALZONES WITH CHEESE AND PESTO
(continued)

Prepare filling while dough rises.

Filling

    2 cups ricotta   **2 cups pesto**

    2 cups grated cheese,   **2 teaspoons dried basil**
      pepperjack or mozzarella

Mix filling ingredients together well.

Final Preparation

Preheat oven to 450 degrees.

Punch down risen dough. Divide into 6 pieces and using a rolling pin, roll out in rounds 1/4-inch thick. Place 1/6 filling onto one side of each calzone. Fold empty half over and pinch edges together to seal filling. Prick to allow steam to escape.

Bake 15-20 minutes, or until calzones are crisp and lightly browned.

CHEESY VEGETABLE LASAGNA

Serves 8   *Bake at 350*

Highly caloric, but when you've gotta, you've gotta.

1 pound spinach lasagna
   noodles
1 tablespoon olive oil
□
1-1/2 pounds pepperjack cheese
1/2 pound provolone
1 pound mozzarella
□
2 pounds ricotta cheese
1 cup grated Pecorino Romano
1/2 teaspoon black pepper
1/2 teaspoon each oregano and thyme
1 teaspoon garlic powder

□
2 cups tomato sauce
□
1 pound vegetables of your
   choice, such as broccoli
   florets, cauliflower florets,
   chopped spinach or sliced
   mushrooms
   or
4 cups ratatouille instead
   of vegetables and tomato
   sauce

Cook lasagna noodles in boiling water for 5 minutes. Rinse in colander under cold water and drain. Put back into pot and add olive oil. Stir to coat to prevent sticking.

Using the shredding disk of a food processor, grate cheeses.

In a large bowl, mix together ricotta, Romano, herbs, garlic and half the cheeses you just grated.

In a 13x9-inch deep baking pan, layer half the lasagna noodles. Cover with ricotta mixture. Spoon vegetables or ratatouille over mixture. Cover with second layer of noodles. Spoon tomato sauce over pasta (skip this if using ratatouille) and spread grated cheese on top. Cover with foil and bake lasagna 45 minutes. Let stand 10 minutes before cutting.

ELBOWS WITH POTATOES AND BASIL

Serves 4-6

A nice, starchy, satisfying combination tinged with basil.

2 cups grated Pecorino Romano	**2 tablespoons dried parsley**
□	□
1/2 cup olive oil	**2 cups tomato sauce**
2 onions, minced	**1 teaspoon salt**
4 medium potatoes, quartered	**1/2 teaspoon pepper**
3 cloves garlic, finely minced	**1/4 teaspoon oregano**
2 tablespoons fresh basil, or 2	□
teaspoons dried	**1 pound elbow pasta**

In a large skillet gently warm olive oil. Add chopped onions, potatoes, garlic, basil and parsley. Saute, stirring frequently, until onions are transparent, about 5 minutes. Add tomato sauce, salt and pepper and oregano.

Cover and simmer over low heat for 20 minutes, or until potatoes are tender when pierced with a knife. Stir occasionally to prevent sticking.

While sauce simmers, bring 4 quarts water to a rollicking boil. Stir in pasta and cook until al dente, about 7 minutes. Drain and place in a deep bowl. Stir in potato mixture.

Serve at once and pass the grated cheese.

GRANDMA SARAH'S FARMER CHEESE BLINTZES

Makes 14-16

Made without flour. Grandma Sarah used bitter almonds from apricot pits to flavor her filling. Serve for breakfast or lunch drizzled with honey and accompanied by fresh berries.

Crepes

6 eggs	**2 tablespoons butter**
1/4 cup water or milk	**for frying**

Beat eggs and water with a fork until foamy. Heat a 10-inch frying pan over medium heat. Add 1/4 teaspoon butter. Turn down flame before pouring in a scant 1/4 cup egg batter. Quickly tilt pan to spread crepe. Patch holes, if any, in blintz with a drop of batter. When blintz underside is lightly browned, turn onto a plate. Do not try to unfold or straighten while hot.

Dot butter in pan and start second blintz. Continue buttering, swirling batter, and dumping crepes onto plate until batter is used. When crepes are cool, straighten and unfold onto a clean plate. Cover with plastic wrap to prevent drying out until filled.

Filling

1 pound farmer cheese (available	**dash cinnamon**
at delicatessen counters)	**1/2 teaspoon vanilla**
6 tablespoons honey	**4 almonds**

Blend filling until almonds are finely ground.

Final Preparation

Place heaping tablespoon of filling on end of blintz nearest you. Fold sides in and roll blintz away, as for egg rolls or stuffed grape leaves. When finished, refrigerate blintzes, covered.

MARUZZINE WITH CAULIFLOWER AND CHEESES

Serves 6-8   *Bake at 350*

Cauliflower, pasta, and melted cheeses create a smooth, rich dish.
Serve with sliced tomatoes and cucumbers.

1/2 cup grated Pecorino Romano
□
**2 pounds maruzzine (shell-shaped
  pasta) cooked and drained**
□
1 pound part-skim mozzarella
1 pound provolone
□
1 pound mushrooms, sliced
1 head cauliflower florets

4 tablespoons olive oil
1/2 teaspoon black pepper
1 teaspoon garlic powder
1/2 teaspoon oregano
1/2 teaspoon basil
1/2 teaspoon marjoram
1 cup tomato sauce
□
parsley sprigs for garnish

Preheat oven to 350 degrees.

Bring 4 quarts water to a rollicking boil and stir in pasta.
Cook until al dente, about 7 minutes. In a colander, rinse pasta
with cold water and drain. Set aside.

Grate mozzarella and provolone using the shredding disk of
a food processor and medium pressure.

In a casserole, combine pasta, mushrooms, cauliflower, olive
oil, grated Romano, mozzarella, provolone, herbs, spices and
sauce. Mix well. Cover with foil and bake casserole 30 minutes.
Uncover and bake another 5 minutes. Serve hot. Garnish with
sprigs of parsley.

MARY'S NOT-SO-HEAVY LASAGNA

Serves 8   *Bake at 350*

Luscious fare on the lighter side!

3 tablespoons olive oil
1 large onion, diced
1 green bell pepper, diced
3 cloves garlic, minced
1 rib celery, diced
1 carrot, diced
1 pound mushrooms, sliced
☐
2 8-ounce cans tomato puree
**16 ounce can whole tomatoes
    with juice**
1 tablespoon basil
1 tablespoon oregano
1 teaspoon salt
1/4 teaspoon crushed red pepper
2 bay leaves
2 tablespoons lite tamari

1/4 cup red wine, optional
☐
12 lasagna noodles
☐
1 pound tofu
**1 pound non-fat cottage
    cheese**
2 egg whites
**1/4 cup Pecorino Romano
    cheese**
1 pound raw spinach, chopped
1 teaspoon black pepper
☐
3 cups sliced zucchini
☐
**8 ounces part-skim mozzarella,
    grated**

Gently warm olive oil in skillet. Saute onion, pepper, garlic, celery, carrot and mushrooms. Add tomato puree, tomatoes, herbs and seasonings. Simmer 1 hour. If you can, refrigerate sauce overnight to give the flavors a chance to blend.

Cook the lasagna noodles in boiling water for 5 minutes. Rinse in colander under cold water and drain.

In a food processor, puree tofu, cottage cheese and egg whites. Stir in Romano, spinach and pepper.

continued . . .

MARY'S NOT-SO-HEAVY LASAGNA
(continued)

To assemble, cover the bottom of a 13x9-inch pan with some sauce. Alternate layers using noodles, cheese and tofu mixture, sliced zucchini, and then more sauce. Repeat twice and end with sauce. Top lasagna with mozzarella cheese.

Bake in a 350 degree oven for 1 hour. Let lasagna sit in pan 10 minutes before cutting to rave reviews.

PIZZA

Makes 3 12-inch pizzas   *Bake at 350, 400*

Herbs and garlic give the crust a wonderful flavor.

2 cups whole wheat pastry flour
2 cups whole wheat bread flour
1 teaspoon salt
☐
2 tablespoons baking yeast
1-1/2 cups lukewarm water
2 teaspoons honey

☐
4 cloves garlic
1/2 cup olive oil
☐
1/2 teaspoon each oregano,
thyme, basil, marjoram

Whirl flour and salt together using the steel blade of a food processor. Sprinkle yeast over lukewarm water and stir to dissolve. Add honey. Pour into workbowl and process by turning motor on/off, 8 times. Add garlic and olive oil. Whirl until dough forms a ball, 15-20 seconds. Add water, a teaspoon at a time, if dough will not form a ball, or a bit more flour if dough is sticky. Add herbs and knead another minute.

Divide dough into three equal pieces. Shape each into a ball and cover. Let rise in a warm, draft-free location for two hours, or until doubled in bulk.

Preheat oven to 350 degrees. Roll each ball out on a greased pizza pan. Press dough out toward edges of the pan with the heel of your hands until dough covers pans thinly. Brush crusts with olive oil and bake 15 minutes.

Remove from oven and top with a favorite sauce, cheeses, and imagination! Turn oven to 400 degrees. Bake pizzas 15 minutes. Let stand 10 minutes before serving to cries of delight.

continued . . .

PIZZA TOPPINGS

anchovy fillets
sliced mushrooms
chopped or sliced onions
chopped or slivered green pepper
fresh garlic, minced
oil-cured black olives
hot chiles
thinly minced Fakin' Bacon or tempeh
pesto

PIZZA SAUCE

4 cups tomato puree
4 tablespoons olive oil
1/4 teaspoon thyme
1/4 teaspoon black pepper
1/4 teaspoon cayenne pepper

1/4 teaspoon oregano
1/4 teaspoon marjoram
1/4 teaspoon basil
1/2 teaspoon garlic powder

Stir pizza sauce ingredients together and simmer over low heat for 15 minutes.

ASSEMBLING PIZZAS

Brush pizza crust with olive oil and cover with sauce (amount to taste). Spread over pizzas a combination of 2 cups grated cheeses - mozzarella and scamorze, thinly sliced gorgonzola, provolone, fontina, pepperjack, or goat cheeses. Sprinkle with freshly grated Romano cheese. Decorate with favorite combination of pizza toppings.

Alternatively, omit tomato sauce and go right onto toppings. Use lots of fresh garlic.

POLENTA PIE

Serves 8   *Bake at 350*

Polenta
- 1 cup cornmeal
- 1/2 cup corn grits
- 3 cups water

- 2 tablespoons olive oil
- 1 teaspoon black pepper
- 1/4 cup grated Pecorino cheese

Filling
- 1/4 cup olive oil
- 4 cloves garlic
- 4 cups chopped onions
- 2 medium carrots, diced
- 4 celery stalks, diced
- 3 tablespoons dried basil
- 2 teaspoons dried oregano
- 1 teaspoon black pepper

☐
- 2 red bell peppers, diced
- 2 medium zucchini, diced
- 1 cup pureed tomatoes

☐
- 2 cups grated melting cheese of choice, (12 ounces) cheddar, pepperjack, etc.

Bring water to a boil. Add cornmeal and corn grits, stirring with a wire whisk until no lumps remain. Add olive oil, pepper, and allow polenta to simmer 10 minutes. Stir often to prevent sticking. Remove from heat and spoon into greased 12x17 baking pan. Cool polenta while preparing filling.

In a large skillet, gently warm olive oil. Saute garlic and onions until tender. Add carrots, celery, herbs and spices. Simmer 5 minutes. Carrots will begin to soften. Add peppers, zucchini, and tomato puree and simmer another 5 minutes. Spoon vegetables onto polenta. Top with grated cheese and bake uncovered at 350 degrees for 30 minutes.

Allow casserole to rest 15 minutes before cutting to serve.

RATATOUILLE FRENCH BREAD PIZZAS

Makes 6 pizzas   *Bake at 350*

Whole wheat French bread topped with ratatouille and spicy pepperjack cheese. Soy cheese works fine too.

1/4 cup olive oil
1 large onion, chopped
4 cloves garlic, minced
1 medium eggplant, unpeeled,
    cut into 1/2-inch cubes
2 small zucchini, diced
1 red bell pepper, chopped
    ☐
1/4 cup pitted olives, chopped
2 cups tomatoes, chopped

1/2 teaspoon black pepper
pinch cayenne pepper
1 teaspoon dried basil
1/2 teaspoon oregano
1/2 teaspoon thyme
    ☐
1 whole wheat French bread,
    sliced in half lengthwise,
    then crosswise into three

4 cups, about 16 ounces, grated cheese of choice:
perhaps provolone, mozzarella, and pepperjack cheeses

Gently warm olive oil in a skillet. Saute onion and garlic until softened, about 5 minutes. Add eggplant, zucchini, and bell pepper. Saute 5 minutes. Cover and simmer until vegetables are tender, 10 minutes. Add olives, tomatoes, pepper and herbs. Simmer, uncovered, until most of liquid evaporates and mixture thickens, about 15 minutes.

Arrange bread on baking sheet. Spread 1 cup grated cheese over bread. Top with ratatouille and then with remaining cheese.

Bake pizzas until cheese is bubbly. Serve piping hot.

SPAGHETTI WITH ARTICHOKE HEARTS

Serves 4-6

A lovely pasta dish. Accompany with a tossed green salad and sliced peaches for dessert.

1/2 cup grated Pecorino Romano cheese	☐
	1 teaspoon salt
1/2 cup olive oil	1/2 teaspoon pepper
2 small onions, minced	1/4 teaspoon oregano
2 cloves garlic, pressed	1 can (28 ounces) plum
1/2 pound mushrooms, thickly sliced	tomatoes
8 ounces artichoke hearts (water packed or frozen)	☐
	1-1/2 pounds spaghetti

In a skillet, gently warm olive oil. Add onions, garlic, mushrooms and artichoke hearts. Simmer, stirring as needed, 10 minutes. Sprinkle with seasonings. Add tomatoes with liquid, mashing as you add them. Bring sauce to a boil, lower heat and simmer 1 hour uncovered.

When sauce is almost done, bring 4 quarts water to a boil, add pasta and cook until al dente, about 7 minutes.

Drain pasta and place in a large bowl. Spoon over half the sauce and toss gently.

Serve immediately with remaining sauce ladled on top. Pass the grated cheese.

SPAGHETTI WITH OLIVE OIL AND GARLIC

Serves 4

The simplest and most delicious way of all to eat pasta.

1 cup grated Pecorino Romano
1/2 cup olive oil
4 cloves garlic
1/2 teaspoon dried basil
1/2 teaspoon oregano

1/2 teaspoon black pepper
1/4 teaspoon red pepper
□
1 pound spaghetti

In a skillet, gently warm olive oil over low heat. Crush garlic with a garlic press and add to oil. Warm until garlic is golden, but be careful not to burn. Add basil, oregano, and pepper. Turn off heat.

Bring 4 quarts water to a rollicking boil. Add spaghetti and stir gently. When pasta is al dente, firm to the tooth, about 7 minutes, drain and place in a large bowl or onto individual plates. Pour oil with garlic and herbs over pasta. Mix gently.

Serve immediately and pass grated cheese.

SPAGHETTI WITH WHITE CLAM SAUCE

Serves 4

Clams infused with garlic and olive oil atop spaghetti.

*1/2 cup grated Pecorino Romano
 cheese*
1/2 cup olive oil
1 large onion, chopped
4 cloves garlic, minced
 ☐
8 ounces chopped clams

several sprigs parsley, chopped
1/4 teaspoon cayenne pepper
1/2 teaspoon black pepper
1-1/2 cups bottled clam juice
 ☐
1 pound spaghetti

In a skillet, gently warm olive oil over medium heat. Saute onion and garlic, stirring as needed, until the onion is transparent, about 5 minutes. Add clams, liquid and all, parsley, red and black pepper, and clam juice to skillet. Bring sauce to a boil. Reduce heat and simmer, uncovered, 15 minutes.

While the sauce is simmering, bring 4 quarts water to a rollicking boil and cook pasta until al dente, firm to the tooth. Test after 7 minutes by biting. Drain and place pasta in a large bowl or on individual plates. Pour sauce over pasta and serve immediately. Pass the grated cheese!

SPINACH FRITADA

Serves 12-16   *Bake at 350*

A snap to prepare, spinach fritada is delicious hot, warm, or cold.

3 pounds spinach, chopped
☐
4 slices whole wheat bread
4 cups grated cheddar,
  pepperjack, mozzarella, or
  other cheese
12 eggs

2 pounds ricotta, cottage
  or farmers' cheese
1/2 cup Pecorino Romano
  cheese
1 teaspoon black pepper
1/2 teaspoon nutmeg

Preheat oven to 350 degrees.   Grease a 12x17 baking dish.

Place chopped spinach in a large mixing bowl.

Using the steel blade of a food processor, blend bread into crumbs.   Add eggs, ricotta, 2 cups grated cheese, pepper and nutmeg.   Add cheese and egg mixture to chopped spinach and mix well.   Spoon mixture into baking pan.   Cover with remaining grated cheese and bake 45 minutes, or until top is golden and firm to the touch.

Remove fritada from oven and let sit for 15 minutes before cutting to serve.

TAMALE PIE

Serves 8   *Bake at 350*

A crunchy crust with spiced beans and a melted cheese topping.

Filling

1 tablespoon olive oil
1 onion, chopped
2 cloves garlic, minced
4 cups diced tomatoes
1 green pepper, chopped
1 cup tomato puree

1 tablespoon chili powder
1-1/2 teaspoons salt
1/4 cup sliced olives
4 cups cooked beans (kidney, lima, or black turtle are nice)

Crust

3 cups water
1/2 cup corn grits
1/2 cup cornmeal

1 tablespoon olive oil
1 tablespoon Pecorino Romano cheese

2 cups grated cheese or soy cheese of your choice (one that melts well)

For the filling, gently warm olive oil in a skillet. Saute onions and garlic until soft, about 5 minutes. Add tomatoes, pepper, tomato puree, chili powder, salt and olives and simmer mixture 10 minutes. Add beans and simmer another 10.

For the crust, bring the water to a boil. Stir in corn grits and cornmeal. Whisk until no lumps remain. Add olive oil and Romano. Simmer 10 minutes. Stir often to prevent sticking.

Grease a 2-quart casserole and spoon in cornmeal crust, reserving 1-1/2 cups for topping. Spread filling over crust and remaining cornmeal over the top. Place grated cheese over all. Bake 30 minutes at 350. Let stand 10 minutes before serving.

Bean and Grain Main Dishes

Back at Kallimos . . .

Bill and I [Jude] had done the math earlier. If Hannah had come to Kallimos about eighty years ago and Haleigh was already a young woman then, that would put Haleigh at or near the century mark. I felt honored that Hannah asked me to work with Haleigh in the garden. A woman of her years would need someone to take care of her.

My heart was singing with what I now recognize was an unhealthy mixture of pride and compassion when I walked into the garden that first morning. I saw an old woman kneeling alongside a patch of vegetables. As there was no one else in sight, I walked up and knelt down beside her. Speaking slowly and distinctly, I introduced myself. She looked at me as if I were some kind of bug.

"Give me your hands, girl," she ordered.

continued . . .

I thought she wanted to hold hands, so I reached out to take hers into mine. She grabbed my hands and turned them palm up. "Worse than I thought," she muttered, rolling her eyes as she stood up. . . . "It's a mystery of the universe how you ever got yourself a bellyful of food with hands like those. . . . They're soft, girl, and more than likely the rest of you is soft, too."

This woman would take some getting used to, I decided. I'd never met a person so old and still so full of vinegar. Hannah speaks softly and has manners to match. Haleigh hollers. Subtlety is unknown to her.

Within five minutes of our initial meeting, Haleigh had marched me to the bean patch and set me to work weeding. While she toted basket after basket of peas to her front porch, I wilted under the glow of the midmorning sun. Tiny bugs with a nasty bite swarmed around my face and arms. My back throbbed. I was thirsty and tired.

The sun was high in the sky, and I was still on my hands and knees when she came back to check on me. I had stuck it out. I hadn't complained, and I'd accomplished more than a little. Unfortunately, I had also pulled up half the bean crop along with the weeds. Haleigh exploded when she saw the devastation I had wrecked. She spit curses and hurled insults. She stamped her feet and wailed. All I could do was cry.

As suddenly as it had started, her tantrum stopped. She looked down at me, at the piles of withered bean seedlings, at me again, and then she laughed. Somewhere in this disaster, she had found some kind of absurd humor. Her laughter was as full-bodied and rich as her fury. The guffaw seemed to rise from her toes. Her body rocked with gales of laughter, and tears came to her eyes. Struggling to contain herself, the old woman I had imagined myself taking care of pulled me to my feet, put her arm around my shoulders, and tousled my hair. She led me to her cottage and, recognizing how tired I was, made a place for me to lie down. While I slept, she sat on the front porch and shelled four baskets of peas.

Adapted from Learning from Hannah © *William H. Thomas, M.D.*

BARLEY WITH RUSSIAN WALNUT SAUCE AND COLORED PEPPERS

Serves 8-10

Barley is one of the oldest grains on earth. Walnut sauce is wonderful over any grain, or even over pasta, fish or poultry.

Walnut Sauce
- **2 heaping cups walnuts**
- **1 teaspoon salt**
- **4 cloves garlic**
- **1 teaspoon coriander**
- **1/2 teaspoon fenugreek seeds**
- **1/4 teaspoon turmeric**
- **1/2 teaspoon paprika**
- **6 teaspoons cider vinegar**
- **1-1/2 cups water**

- **9 cups water**
- **3 cups barley**
- ☐
- **2 tablespoons olive oil**
- **2 red bell peppers, sliced**
- **2 green bell peppers, sliced**
- **2 yellow bell peppers, sliced**
- ☐
- **parsley for garnish**
- **walnut halves for garnish**

Using the steel blade of a food processor, blend walnuts, salt, garlic, coriander, fenugreek, turmeric and paprika until smooth. Run the machine and drizzle in vinegar and enough water to make a sauce the consistency of light cream. Transfer sauce to a bowl, cover and refrigerate for at least an hour, allowing the flavors to blend.

In the meantime, bring water to a boil and add barley. Lower heat, cover pot and simmer 50 minutes, or until barley is tender.

In a skillet, warm olive oil and saute peppers until they begin to wilt but are still brilliant in color.

To serve, mound barley on individual plates. Place peppers to the side, top with walnut sauce and garnish plates with parsley and walnut pieces.

BLACK BEAN, CORN AND SWEET POTATO STEW

Serves 6

Satisfying, easy to prepare. Serve with crusty brown bread and a green salad. Mangoes and berries would make a light dessert.

2 sweet potatoes, cubed	**1 teaspoon basil**
□	**1 teaspoon oregano**
2 tablespoons olive oil	**2 teaspoons salt**
1 large onion, chopped	**1/2 teaspoon cayenne pepper**
4 cloves garlic, minced	□
2 green peppers, chopped	**3 cups cooked black beans**
1 jalapeno pepper, seeded and	□
finely minced	**2 cups corn kernels, fresh**
1 cup diced tomatoes	**or frozen**
1/4 cup dried parsley	

Steam sweet potato in 2 cups water until tender, but not over cooked. Drain and set aside.

Gently warm olive oil in a large skillet. Saute onion and garlic until onion is soft, about 5 minutes. Add peppers, tomato, parsley, herbs, salt and cayenne. Saute another 5 minutes.

Add sweet potatoes, black beans and corn to skillet. Cover and simmer stew until hot, 10 minutes. If stew starts to stick or burn, add a few tablespoons water.

Gently stir to mix. Taste, adjust seasonings, cover pot, and let stew stand 10 minutes for flavors to blend.

EGGPLANT, PASTA AND CHICKPEA STEW

Serves 8

Beans and pasta, topped with an eggplant sauce make a satisfying combination.

4 tablespoons olive oil	1/2 teaspoon black pepper
2 large onions, chopped	1/2 teaspoon oregano
6 cloves garlic, minced	1/2 teaspoon cayenne pepper
1 green pepper, chopped	(optional)
☐	☐
1 large eggplant, peeled and cubed in 1" pieces	2 cups chickpeas, cooked or canned (if canned, drained)
☐	☐
2 cups chopped tomatoes	2 cups elbow macaroni of your
1-1/2 teaspoons salt	choice

Gently warm olive oil in a skillet. Saute onion, garlic and green pepper for 5 minutes. Add eggplant and saute another 10 minutes, stirring occasionally. Add tomatoes, seasonings, herbs, and chickpeas to stew. Cover and simmer 30 minutes. Watch carefully. If stew appears to be sticking, add a little boiling water.

While stew simmers, bring a large pot of water to a boil and cook pasta until al dente, about 7 minutes. Drain pasta and stir into stew. Taste, adjust seasoning and serve hot or cold.

FAVA—MIDDLE EASTERN YELLOW SPLIT PEAS

Serves 12

There's something luscious about the combination of yellow split peas with garlic, olive oil and cumin.

4 cups yellow split peas	**1/2 teaspoon cayenne pepper**
□	**1/2 teaspoon cumin**
1/2 cup olive oil	**1 teaspoon salt**
1 large onion, chopped	**1 teaspoon black pepper**
4 cloves garlic, minced	□
	chopped parsley for garnish

Using a mesh colander, rinse yellow split peas. Place in heavy pot with water to cover by 3 inches. Simmer on low until peas are tender, about an hour. Check and add water if necessary to prevent mixture from sticking.

Gently warm olive oil in a large skillet and saute onion and garlic. When split peas are soft and mushy, add to skillet. Stir until onions and garlic are well incorporated and then add remaining seasonings to taste.

Serve garnished with parsley.

Fava may be served like houmous, with pita and vegetables, or it may be used as an accompaniment to fish, chicken or meat instead of potatoes or rice.

GREEK STEW WITH POTATOES, TOMATOES, PEPPER AND TOFU

Serves 8

A terrific Greek stew with tofu instead of fish.

**2 pounds firm tofu, cubed and
  marinated in 1-1/2 tbs.
  lemon juice**
  ☐
**8 medium baking potatoes, cut
  lengthwise into spears**
  ☐
1/2 cup olive oil
1 large onion, chopped
2 large garlic cloves, minced
2 green peppers, sliced

4 cups tomatoes, diced
1/2 cup fresh parsley, chopped
1 teaspoon oregano
4 bay leaves
1 tablespoon paprika
1 teaspoon black pepper
  ☐
1/2 cup cider vinegar
  ☐
salt to taste

Cube tofu and marinate in lemon juice while preparing the remainder of the dish.

Steam potatoes until tender, about 15-20 minutes.

While potatoes steam, gently warm olive oil. Saute onion and garlic until softened, about 5 minutes. Add green pepper and saute another few minutes. Add tomatoes, parsley, oregano, bay leaves, paprika and black pepper, and simmer, uncovered, 15 minutes, or until potatoes are ready.

Add cider vinegar, steamed potatoes, and tofu to sauce. Cover, turn off heat, and let stew stand 10 minutes to give the flavors a chance to blend. Taste, adjust seasoning and serve.

INDIAN PLATTER

Serves 12

An exotic, Indian sampler with three entrees served side-by-side. Garnish with lemon slices and parsley.

Cauliflower with Basmati Rice

1 cup basmati rice	*1/2 teaspoon hot pepper flakes*
2 cups water	*1 teaspoon turmeric*
□	*2 tablespoons water*
2 tablespoons olive oil	*1 large head cauliflower broken*
1 teaspoon cumin seeds	*into florets*
1 tablespoon coriander seeds	*salt, optional*

Bring water to a boil, add rice and lower heat. Simmer covered for 45 minutes, while remainder of meal is being prepared.

Gently warm olive oil in a skillet. Add cumin, coriander, hot pepper flakes, turmeric, water and cauliflower. Cover and cook on low until cauliflower is tender. Add salt, if desired, to taste. Toss in cooked Basmati rice.

Indian Spinach

2 pounds spinach, finely	*1 teaspoon chili powder*
chopped	*1 teaspoon coriander*
4 tablespoons olive oil	*1 teaspoon lemon juice*
4 cloves garlic, finely minced	*1 teaspoon salt*
1 teaspoon cumin	

Gently warm olive oil in a skillet and stir in garlic and all spices and seasoning. Saute 2 minutes. Add spinach. Stir and cook until spinach is hot.

continued . . .

INDIAN PLATTER
(continued)

Lentils with Curry Sauce

2 cups green lentils
4 cups water
1 cup curry sauce

lemon to taste
salt and pepper to taste

Bring water to a boil, add lentils and cook 15 minutes, or until lentils are tooth-tender, but not mushy. Add curry sauce, lemon, salt and pepper to taste.

To serve, place some of each entree on dinner plates. Or, put each entree on a serving platter and let people help themselves buffet style.

Curry Sauce, about 6 cups

1/4 cup olive oil
8-10 pasilla or poblano whole dried red chiles
8 cloves garlic
1 large Spanish onion, quartered

2 tablespoons lemon juice
2 teaspoons curry powder
2 teaspoons salt
4 cups tomato sauce

In a large skillet, gently warm olive oil. Add dried chiles, stirring constantly for 5 minutes. Spoon chiles onto cutting board to cool. Cut stems and tops off and shake out most of the seeds. (Heat is in the seeds, so for a hot sauce, leave more in. Poblano and pasilla chiles are not hot, HOT peppers.)

Using the steel blade of a food processor, blend peppers, garlic and onion, together with lemon juice, curry powder, salt and tomato sauce. Scrape sauce back into skillet with a rubber spatula. Simmer 10 minutes.

Remove the one cup of sauce needed for this recipe and refrigerate or freeze the rest for future use. Curry sauce keeps for two months under refrigeration.

ITALIAN EGGPLANT WITH NUTS AND SEEDS

Serves 4   *Bake at 350*

This recipe was given to us by Barbara Shoemaker and Bob Larkin who adapted it from a dish made by Carol Priest, a friend of theirs from California. Barbara says the secret is the vinegar.

1/2 cup cashew pieces
1/2 cup sunflower seeds
☐
1 medium eggplant, sliced
* in 1/2 inch slices*
1/2 cup olive oil
1 onion, chopped
2 ribs celery, diced

1 large green pepper, chopped
3 tablespoons dried parsley
3 cloves garlic, minced
☐
1 cup tomato sauce
1/3 cup wine vinegar
pepper to taste

Preheat oven to 350 degrees. Roast cashews and sunflower seeds on a cookie sheet for 10 minutes. Remove to cool.

Bake sliced eggplant until tender, about 15 minutes. Cut into cubes. (This step can be eliminated. Eggplant can be cubed and sauteed along with remaining vegetables. Doing so will result in a softer, wetter eggplant.)

Gently warm olive oil in a skillet. Saute onion, celery, green pepper, parsley and garlic about 5 minutes.

Add eggplant, tomato sauce and vinegar. Simmer, covered, for 15 minutes. Add pepper to taste. Stir in toasted cashews and sunflower seeds.

Serve over steamed brown rice.

KIDNEY BEAN STEW WITH MILLET PILAF

Serves 6

Millet, an important grain in Indian and African cooking, has a pleasant, nutty flavor. Here it goes Italian!

1-1/2 cups millet	1 jalapeno pepper, seeded, and
3 cups water	minced
1/2 teaspoon salt	☐
☐	1 teaspoon basil
2 tablespoons olive oil	1 teaspoon oregano
2 onions, chopped	3 cups cooked kidney beans
4 carrots, sliced	2 cups diced tomatoes
1 red bell pepper, diced	salt and pepper to taste
1 green bell pepper, diced	chopped parsley for garnish

Toast millet in a dry saucepan over medium heat for 5 minutes, stirring constantly. Grains will brown slightly and begin to pop. Add water and salt, and bring to a boil. Cover saucepan and turn down heat. Simmer millet 30 minutes, until water has been absorbed.

Meanwhile, prepare stew. Gently warm oil in a large skillet. Saute onions, carrots, and peppers. Cover and cook 15 minutes, or until carrots are tender. Stir from time to time.   Add herbs, cooked beans and tomatoes. Taste and adjust seasoning.

Place millet on each plate and spoon kidney bean mixture in the center. Garnish with chopped parsley.

Alternatively, millet and kidney bean mixture may be stirred together and served in bowls.

LATKES

Serves 4

Potato pancakes - potatoes and onions sizzling in oil - made at Chanukah taste as wonderful as they smell. Start a second batch as soon as the first is off the griddle or out of the frying pan. People eat their weight in latkes!

6 medium potatoes, scrubbed but UNPEELED
3 onions, quartered
1 unbeaten egg

1 teaspoon salt
1 teaspoon black pepper
peanut oil for frying

Grate potatoes and onions with the fine shredding disk of a food processor. (Watch the knuckles if you grate by hand.)

Mix grated potatoes and onions, egg, salt and pepper in a bowl. Drop batter by large spoonfuls into a frying pan with hot oil barely deep enough to cover latkes, or make them on a well buttered pancake griddle heated for griddlecakes. Pour a small amount of oil around each pancake as it sizzles on the griddle. Brown latkes on both sides for either method.

The batter will become soupy in the bowl as it stands. Rather than draining or squeezing liquid out, or adding flour to absorb it, just stir it back into batter before using.

Drain latkes on absorbent paper and serve hot - plain, with applesauce, or sour cream.

MEXICAN TAMALE PEPPERS

Serves 12   *Bake at 350*

A filling so flavorful, it needs no cheese! Serve with a marinated vegetable salad and honeydew melon for dessert.

1/4 cup olive oil
4 cloves garlic, chopped
2 large onions, chopped
    ☐

3 tablespoons chili powder
2 teaspoons ground cumin
2 cups masa harina, or very fine
    cornmeal

6 cups chopped tomatoes,
    with liquid
1 teaspoon salt
    ☐

4 cups cooked pink beans
1 pound corn kernels
    ☐
12 large green bell peppers

Gently warm olive oil in a large skillet. Saute onion and garlic until soft, about 5 minutes. Add chili and cumin and then stir in tomatoes, masa harina, and salt. Cook, stirring until mixture is thick, about 5 minutes. Stir in beans and corn. Stir another 5 minutes.

Preheat oven to 350 degrees.

Slice tops from peppers, remove seeds and tough inner ribs. Spoon cornmeal mixture into peppers and place them upright in a baking dish. Cover pan with foil and bake peppers 40 minutes, or until tender.

If desired, serve peppers with a spoonful of salsa on top.

MILLET IN A NEST OF VEGETABLES WITH TOMATO COULIS

Serves 4

Millet with colorful, sauteed vegetables and a spicy tomato coulis.

Vegetables and Millet

2 cups millet
4 cups water
1 teaspoon salt
□
1 stalk celery, julienned
1 onion, diced
1 large carrot, julienned
1 large zucchini, julienned

1 yellow crookneck squash, julienned
□
1 tablespoon olive oil
2 cloves garlic, crushed
1 teaspoon black pepper
salt to taste

Tomato Coulis

2 cups tomatoes, diced
2 cloves garlic, minced
1 teaspoon red pepper flakes

1 tablespoon cider vinegar
1 teaspoon dried basil
salt and pepper to taste

Bring water and salt to a boil. Stir in millet, lower heat, cover pot and simmer 45 minutes.

Steam vegetables until crisp-tender. Warm olive oil in a skillet. Add garlic and stir. Stir in vegetables and black pepper just to coat with oil. Season with salt, if desired. Set aside.

In a pan, simmer tomatoes, garlic, red pepper flakes, vinegar and basil 15 minutes, or until coulis thickens. Adjust seasoning.

Mound 1 cup millet on each plate. Place vegetables decoratively around millet. Make a depression in the center and spoon on tomato coulis. Serve immediately.

RICE PILAF WITH SPINACH AND CANNELLINI

Serves 4

Sun-dried tomatoes, rice, white kidney beans and Pecorino Romano. Serve fresh apricots or peaches for dessert.

1 tablespoon olive oil	8 cups fresh spinach, chopped
1 onion, chopped	1/2 cup freshly grated Pecorino
4 cloves garlic, minced	Romano cheese
1-1/2 cups brown basmati rice	1 teaspoon black pepper
3 cups water or vegetable broth	salt, if desired, to taste
☐	☐
3 cups cooked cannellini beans	3 tablespoons pine nuts
(white kidneys), or 3 cups	1/4 cup oil-packed sun-dried
canned, rinsed and drained	tomatoes, sliced thinly

Gently warm olive oil in a large skillet. Saute onion and garlic until onion is golden, about 5-7 minutes. Reduce heat and stir in rice until opaque, about 3 minutes. Add water and bring to boil. Cover skillet and simmer until rice is tender, about 45 minutes.

When rice is cooked, mix in beans, spinach, Romano and black pepper. Cover and continue cooking until thoroughly heated, usually several minutes.

Taste and adjust seasoning. Remove pilaf to serving platter and garnish with pine nuts and sun-dried tomatoes.

SPICY STUFFED EGGPLANT

Serves 6   *Bake at 375*

A colorful, fragrant twist to a classic. Potatoes and tofu replace the heavy meat and cheese filling that is often used. Serve with a red leaf lettuce salad and follow with fruit of the season.

3 medium eggplants	*1/2 teaspoon cayenne*
4 cups cubed potatoes	*1/4 teaspoon cloves*
1 pound silken tofu	☐
☐	*2 medium carrots, diced*
2 tablespoons olive oil	*1 tablespoon lemon juice*
4 garlic cloves, minced	*1 green pepper, diced*
2 cups chopped onions	*1 cup string beans, in 2" pieces*
2 teaspoons ground cumin	☐
1 teaspoon tumeric	*2 cups cooked chickpeas*

Slice eggplants in half lengthwise, leaving stems on. Place cut side down on an oiled baking sheet. Cover and bake at 375 degrees until tender, about 30-40 minutes. While eggplant is baking, boil potatoes until tender. Drain. Using a food processor, blend potatoes with tofu.

Gently warm olive oil in a skillet and saute onions, garlic and spices until onions are translucent. Add carrots and lemon juice. Simmer 5 minutes before adding pepper and string beans to cook an additional 5 minutes. Combine vegetables with potato.

Turn baked eggplant halves over in baking pan. With a fork or spoon, mash pulp, taking care not to break the skin. Push aside some of the pulp, making a hollow in each half. Divide filling and mound on each half. Bake covered 15 minutes, then uncovered for an additional 15-20 minutes.

Serve with chickpeas on the side. Sprinkle with black pepper.

VEGETABLE PAELLA WITH ABORIO RICE

Serves 6

Aborio rice, an Italian short-grain rice typically used in risotto, together with vegetables, makes a colorful dish. Short-grain brown rice works beautifully too.

1/2 cup water	*2 cups chopped tomatoes*
2 carrots, halved lengthwise	*1/4 teaspoon saffron*
and sliced	*3 cups water*
1/4 pound green beans,	*1 teaspoon salt*
cut into 2" lengths	*1/2 teaspoon cayenne pepper*
□	□
4 tablespoons olive oil	*1 cup slivered almonds*
1 large onion, chopped	*1/2 cup dried parsley*
6 cloves garlic, minced	*1 cup green peas*
1 large green and red,	*2 zucchini, halved and sliced*
pepper chopped	□
1 jalapeno pepper, minced	*soy granules, optional*
2 cups aborio rice	*whole almonds, for garnish*

Steam carrots in 1/2 cup water until crisp-tender. Place in colander and cool under water. Drain. Set aside. Steam green beans the same way. Cool under water, drain and set aside.

Gently warm olive oil in skillet and saute onion, garlic, and peppers 3 minutes. Add rice and stir until translucent, a minute or two. Add tomatoes and saffron and simmer 5 minutes. Add water, salt and cayenne, and bring paella to a boil. Cover and simmer 40 minutes, until rice is tooth-tender.

Stir in slivered almonds, parsley, peas, carrots, string beans and zucchini. Cover skillet and let paella stand for a few minutes. If rice is wet, stir in several tablespoons soy granules to absorb excess moisture.

VEGETARIAN CHILI

Makes 8 cups to serve 6

Love chili? You'll love this! Serve this way, or over steamed brown rice. Blended, this chili makes a superb filling in tortillas for burritos. Use a dollop to accompany turkey tacos.

6 cups cooked beans - pinto, kidney, red beans, chickpeas, black beans - all are good, mix and match
☐
2 tablespoons olive oil
2 large onions, chopped
4 garlic cloves, minced
2 tablespoons chili powder
2 teaspoons ground cumin

☐
1 pound carrots, halved lengthwise and sliced
2 cups diced tomatoes
1 green pepper, diced
1 red pepper, diced
1 jalapeno pepper, seeded and minced fine
☐
1 teaspoon salt
1/2 teaspoon oregano

Gently warm olive oil in a soup kettle and saute onion and garlic until onion is softened. Add chili powder and cumin and stir 1 minute. Add carrots, diced tomatoes with their liquid, and peppers. Cover and simmer chili until carrots are tender, stirring occasionally, about 10 minutes.

Add beans to pot and simmer chili, covered, 15 minutes without stirring. Turn off heat, add salt and oregano, and mix chili so carrots are well distributed. Cover pot again and let chili stand 30 minutes to give flavors a chance to blend.

Taste, adjust seasoning and serve.

Poultry Main Dishes

Back at Kallimos . . .

[Hannah] pointed to a patch of exuberant, lemon-colored flowers that sprang from their stalks like upturned bells. "Look at those flowers," she said. The flowers crowded around us like a flock of hungry chickens. "They are meant to live in the moist, shady soil that surrounds great trees like this one. Only a fool would plant them in the open or in dry soil. Though they are often tempted to forget it, human beings are much like these flowers. We are meant to live in a world that revolves around plants, animals, and children. So it has been since human beings first walked this Earth, and so it will always be. Your machines and your science will never change this."

Jude spoke up. "At home, most people consider plants, animals, and children to be pleasant distractions from the real business of living. Millions of people have pets, millions more enjoy gardening, and almost every neighborhood has a park or play-

continued . . .

ground where you can watch children play. But what you're saying, I think, is that these things should be at the center of our lives, that we need to change the focus."

Excerpted from Learning from Hannah © *William H. Thomas, M.D.*

ARTICHOKE, CHICKPEA AND FENNEL GIAMBOTTA

Serves 8

An Italian stew which incorporates a unique blend of herbs, chicken, artichoke hearts, and chickpeas. Have fun with this recipe. To make it vegetarian, add firm tofu (2 pounds) instead of chicken. Or add cubes of potatoes or sweet potatoes instead of the chicken.

8 chicken thighs or breasts
2 teaspoons dried basil
2 teaspoons dried parsley
4 cloves garlic, minced
3 plum tomatoes
2 red bell-peppers, chopped coarsely
1 large zucchini, halved, sliced in 1-inch pieces
1 fennel bulb, halved, sliced, or 1 teaspoon dried fennel seed

1/2 teaspoon each thyme, oregano, black and red pepper
2 bay leaves
1-1/2 teaspoons salt
4 cups cooked, drained chickpeas or use other beans such as lima
2 tablespoons olive oil
1 teaspoon wine vinegar
8 artichoke hearts

Broil chicken until crisp and brown, about 15-20 minutes. Set aside while preparing the remainder of the dish.

Place herbs, chopped garlic and diced tomatoes in a large flame-proof casserole or kettle. Add red pepper and fennel. Mix in chickpeas together with 1 cup of their stock, olive oil, wine vinegar, and artichoke hearts. Bring to a boil. Add chicken, cover, and simmer over low heat for 15-20 minutes, or until the chicken is tender.

Remove bay leaves and stir in zucchini. Serve to oohs and aahs.

This stew also works beautifully with a firm white fish such as haddock. Simply add fish to stew during the last 10 minutes.

CHICKEN AND SHRIMP JAMBALAYA

Serves 4

From steamy New Orleans comes this lively and aromatic dish. Bring on the jazz band!

2 tablespoons olive oil
4 ribs celery, sliced
1 large onion, chopped
4 cloves garlic, minced
1 green pepper, chopped
1 6-ounce package Fakin' Bacon,*
*   chopped*
2 cups boneless chicken, cut in
*   bite-sized pieces*
1 cup raw short-grain
*   brown rice*

2 cups tomatoes, chopped,
*   liquid drained*
1 8-ounce bottle clam juice
1 cup water
1/2 teaspoon thyme
3 bay leaves
1/2 pound shrimp, shelled and
*   deveined*
1 bunch scallions
salt and pepper to taste

Gently warm olive oil in a large skillet and saute celery, onion, garlic and pepper together with Fakin' Bacon and chicken until vegetables are tender and bacon is nicely browned. Add rice and stir one minute. Add tomatoes and their liquid, together with clam juice, water, bay leaves and thyme.

Simmer, covered until rice has cooked, about 45 minutes. Add shrimp and cook until they turn pink, about 3-4 minutes. Add chopped green onions and stir in gently.

Taste, adjust seasonings and serve hot!

*Fakin' Bacon is a soy product which has a smoky flavor. Use it in any recipe which calls for ham or bacon. You can find it in any natural food store. We love it in paella, bean soups, etc.

CHICKEN CON MOLE VERDE

Serves 6-8   *Bake at 350*

Chicken with a deliciously fragrant Mexican sauce. Tomatillos are a Mexican paper-husked green tomato, which are easily grown in home gardens anywhere tomatoes can be grown! Serve with boiled rice or barley or millet.

3 pounds boneless chicken   **2 large dried ancho chiles**
1 large onion, chopped   **2 cloves garlic**
6 garlic cloves, minced   **1/4 cup dried parsley**
1 teaspoon salt   ☐
        ☐   **3 tablespoons olive oil**
1/2 cup pumpkin seeds   **1/2 teaspoon salt**
        ☐   **1/2 teaspoon cumin**
1-1/2 pounds tomatillos, husked

Mix chicken with onion, garlic and salt. Bake in a 350 degree oven until chicken juice runs clear when meat is pierced with a knife, about 30 minutes.

To dry-roast pumpkin seeds, stir in a hot pan until lightly browned, 2-3 minutes. Cool slightly.

Place husked tomatillos in a saucepan with water to cover. Bring to a boil and cook 10 minutes. Drain and cool. Combine tomatillos, chiles, 2 cloves garlic, parsley and pumpkin seeds in a food processor. Blend until pumpkin seeds are finely ground.

Gently warm olive oil in a large skillet. Add pumpkin seed sauce. Simmer five minutes. Add chicken, remaining salt and cumin. Simmer uncovered 15 minutes. Spoon out over grain.

CHICKEN CREOLE

Serves 8

Creole cooking - robust, animated by the trinity of onions, celery and green peppers. Serve over artichoke noodles or rice.

8 assorted chicken pieces (i.e., thighs and breasts)
1/4 cup olive oil
2 large onions, chopped
4 cloves garlic, minced
2 ribs celery, sliced
2 green peppers, chopped coarsely
2 cups diced tomatoes
1 lemon, thinly sliced

1/4 teaspoon cayenne pepper
1/4 teaspoon black pepper
1 teaspoon salt
1 teaspoon chili powder
1 teaspoon basil
1/2 teaspoon thyme
4 bay leaves
2 bunches scallions, sliced
2 sprigs parsley

Broil chicken until crisp and brown, about 15-20 minutes. Remove and set aside.

Gently warm olive oil in a heavy Dutch oven or large skillet. Saute onions, garlic, celery and pepper slowly until vegetables begin to change color and become transparent, about 5 minutes. Add tomatoes and cook for another 5 minutes.

Add lemon, cayenne, black pepper, salt, basil, thyme, chili powder and bay leaves. Simmer 15 minutes. Add water if needed. Add chicken to creole mixture and cook 30 minutes, or until chicken is tender.

Remove dish from the stove. Taste and correct seasoning. Garnish with scallions and parsley. Serve with noodles or rice.

CHICKEN MOLE WITH ALMONDS AND SESAME

Serves 6

Mole without chocolate. Thanks to Gabrielle Matuz for the idea!

2 tablespoons olive oil	**3 teaspoons pepper**
2 dried ancho peppers	**1/4 teaspoon cinnamon**
1 dried pasilla pepper	**1 teaspoon salt**
□	□
1 large onion	**3 cups water**
6 cloves garlic	**1-1/2 cups raw brown rice**
2 medium tomatoes	□
2 tablespoons almonds	**1-1/2 pounds 1/2-inch thick**
2 tablespoons sesame seeds	**chicken slices**
1/2 teaspoon cloves	**sesame seeds to garnish**

In a large skillet, gently warm olive oil. Add peppers and stir-fry 5 minutes. Remove peppers from oil and blend in a food processor. Strain to eliminate peel and seeds. Set pepper puree aside.

Using the food processor again, blend onion, garlic, tomato, almonds, sesame seeds and seasonings. Add mixture to same skillet and simmer 10 minutes. If necessary, add a little water to prevent burning. Add pepper puree. Simmer another 5 minutes.

While mole simmers, in a small pot, bring 3 cups water to a boil. Sir in rice. Cover pot, lower heat and simmer rice 45 minutes. Turn heat off and leave cover on until ready to use rice.

Add chicken to sauce in skillet. Cover and simmer 30 minutes. Taste and adjust seasoning. Serve chicken mole over rice. Sprinkle with sesame seeds for garnish.

CHICKEN STEW WITH POTATOES AND TOMATOES

Serves 8   *Bake at 350*

A snap to prepare. Mix everything and pop into the oven!

2 pounds boneless chicken breasts, skinless and cubed
16 small red potatoes, quartered
2 cups coarsely chopped fresh or canned tomatoes
6 cloves garlic, minced
1 teaspoon black pepper

2 teaspoons oregano
1 teaspoon thyme
1 teaspoon marjoram
1/4 cup olive oil
8 ounces mushrooms, sliced
☐
chopped parsley for garnish

Preheat oven to 350 degrees.

Place chicken in an oven-proof casserole. Add potatoes, tomatoes, garlic, pepper, oregano, thyme, marjoram, olive oil and mushrooms. Stir to mix.

Bake, uncovered, 1 hour, or until potatoes are easily pierced with a knife. Baste casserole with its own sauce every 20 minutes. Remove from oven and sprinkle with parsley to serve.

CHICKEN TACOS

Makes 4 generous servings

Kids of ALL ages love these lighter tacos. If ground chicken is not available, substitute ground turkey.

2 tablespoons olive oil	**1/2 teaspoon thyme**
1 large onion, chopped	**1 cup tomato sauce**
4 cloves garlic, minced	**salt and pepper to taste**
☐	☐
2 pounds ground chicken	**corn tortillas**
☐	**2 tomatoes, chopped**
2 teaspoons cumin	**1 avocado, peeled and chopped**
2 teaspoons chili powder	☐
2 jalapeno peppers, minced	**2 cups vegetarian chili**
1/2 teaspoon oregano	

Gently warm olive oil in a large skillet. Saute onions and garlic until onions begin to soften, about 2-3 minutes. Add chicken and saute until nicely browned.

Add spices, peppers and tomato sauce. Simmer 10 minutes. Taste and adjust seasoning.

Spoon taco mixture over a corn tortilla. Top with tomato and avocado. Accompany with a heaping spoonful of vegetarian chili on the side.

CHICKEN WITH 40 CLOVES OF GARLIC

Serves 10   *Bake at 325*

The aroma of garlic permeates the house and makes mouths water. Baked garlic cloves can be pressed, and the garlic, which is buttery and mild, used on bread or potatoes.

5 chicken thighs	2 stalks celery, sliced
5 chicken breast halves	1 teaspoon thyme
40 cloves garlic, unpeeled	1 teaspoon rosemary
and left whole	1 teaspoon tarragon
2 carrots, sliced	1 teaspoon salt
2 kohlrabi, diced	1 teaspoon black pepper
	parsley sprigs, for garnish

Wash and pat chicken dry. Broil until the skin is crisp and brown, about 10 minutes.

Preheat oven to 325 degrees. Place chicken in a roasting pan together with unpeeled garlic cloves, carrots, kohlrabi, celery and herbs. Cover pan with foil, then place a lid over foil. Bake chicken 1-1/2 hours. Uncover during the last 15 minutes. Chicken is done when fork inserted into thigh comes out easily and juice runs clear.

Transfer chicken to a platter. Using slotted spoon, remove cloves of garlic and scatter around platter. Spoon vegetables over chicken. Sprinkle with salt and pepper, if desired.

Serve at once with crusty bread, baked potatoes and a green salad.

EASY CHICKEN CURRY

Serves 8

Serve on a bed of fluffy rice. Basmati rice is especially fragrant.

2 onions, quartered
4 cloves garlic
2 tablespoons lemon juice
1 teaspoon curry powder
1/2 teaspoon red pepper flakes
1 teaspoon salt
1/2 teaspoon ground ginger

1/2 cup tomato sauce or 1 large tomato
☐
3 pounds chicken pieces with skin removed
☐
4 cups cooked garbanzo beans

Using the steel blade of a food processor, blend onions, garlic, lemon juice, curry, red pepper, salt, ginger and tomato. Stop the machine once or twice to scrape down the sides of the workbowl with a rubber spatula.

Remove sauce to a fry pan and stir 3 minutes, until mixture begins to darken attractively.   Add chicken and turn to coat. Cover fry pan and simmer chicken for an hour, stirring once or twice, or until tender. Add chickpeas and cook just until they are heated through.

Serve on a bed of rice garnished with a sprig of parsley or watercress.

As a variation, try tofu or shrimp. Adjust the cooking time accordingly - shrimp until they turn pink, tofu, until heated through.

INDIAN CHICKEN

Serves 8   *Bake at 400*

Flavorful, not spicy. Want more heat, add more red pepper!
Serve with millet or baked potatoes and a cucumber yogurt salad.

8 large garlic cloves
1 large onion, quartered
1 teaspoon ginger
1/2 teaspoon cumin
1 teaspoon chili powder
1/2 teaspoon salt
1/2 teaspoon each red and
  black pepper

1/4 teaspoon ground
  cardamom
  ☐
1 3-4 pound chicken, cut into
  serving pieces
1 lemon

Using the steel blade of a food processor, puree garlic and
onion together with spices. Stop the machine once or twice to
scrape down the sides of the workbowl with a rubber spatula.
When paste is smooth, coat chicken. Cover and marinate for
several hours, or overnight.

Before baking, make a number of small cuts in chicken and
squeeze lemon juice all over.

Roast chicken in a 400 degree oven for 1 hour. Baste several
times with pan juices.

LEMON CHICKEN

Serves 4

The combination of yogurt, lemon, and tomato gives this chicken a distinctive flavor and fragrance. Serve over bulgur or lentils with steamed asparagus or green beans on the side.

4 boneless chicken breasts	**1 onion, quartered**
2 tablespoons yogurt	**4 tomatoes, sliced, for garnish**
1/2 teaspoon salt	**1 green pepper, sliced in rings,**
1/2 teaspoon mustard powder	**for garnish**
2 teaspoons lemon juice	**few sprigs fresh mint or parsley,**
1/2 teaspoon curry powder	**for garnish**

Cut each chicken breast into 8 pieces.

Using the steel blade of a food processor or blender, blend yogurt, salt, mustard, lemon juice, curry and onion. Combine marinade with chicken. Cover and let stand 1 hour.

Broil chicken (or stir-saute in a skillet) until tender and cooked, about 20 minutes.

Transfer to a hot platter, or to individual serving plates. Garnish with tomatoes, green pepper rings and fresh mint or parsley.

MARINATED CHICKEN WITH OREGANO

Serves 8   *Bake at 425*

Serve with a baked potato, steamed cauliflower and carrots. Finish off the meal with a fruit cobbler!

4 pounds cut-up chicken
1/4 cup olive oil
1/4 cup lemon juice
1 teaspoon salt
1 tablespoon oregano

4 cloves garlic mashed with
   garlic press
1 teaspoon black pepper
a few sprigs watercress or
   parsley, for garnish

Place chicken, olive oil, lemon juice, salt, oregano, garlic and black pepper in a large bowl. Mix so chicken is well coated. Refrigerate, covered, for 24 hours.

Preheat grill. Remove chicken from marinade and grill, skin side down. Cook over the lowest heat with the cover down. Turn after 15 minutes and baste with remaining marinade. Grill for another 10-15 minutes.

Marinated chicken may also be baked in a hot, 425-degree oven for 30-45 minutes.

Garnish with a sprig of watercress or parsley.

MIDDLE EASTERN TURKEY BURGERS

Serves 6

A favorite for informal entertaining with each guest putting together her/his own burger.

Turkey Burger
- **2 pounds ground turkey**
- **1 medium onion, minced**
- **2 cloves garlic, minced**
- **1/2 teaspoon oregano**
- **2 tablespoons dried parsley**

- **2 teaspoons cumin**
- **1 teaspoon salt**
- **1 teaspoon black pepper**
- **2 tablespoons rice, wheat or oat bran**

Tahini Dressing
- **1/2 cup sesame tahini**
- **1/4 cup lemon juice**
- **about 1/2 cup water to thin**
- **2 cloves garlic**

- ☐
- **2 tablespoons olive oil**
- **3 cups chopped tomatoes**
- ☐
- **6 whole grain hamburger buns**

Knead burgers together in a mixing bowl and shape. Grill or broil 4-5 minutes on each side.

Using the steel blade of a food processor or a blender, blend tahini, lemon, garlic and water. Dressing should be the consistency of heavy cream. If it is too thick, add a few more spoonfuls of water. Taste dressing and adjust seasoning.

Mix chopped tomatoes with a little olive oil.

To serve, place turkey burgers on bun. Spoon dressing and chopped tomatoes on top.

PERSIAN STUFFED EGGPLANT

Serves 8   *Bake at 375*

A distinctive dish with a flavorful stuffing, which may also be used to stuff zucchini, peppers, or tomatoes, or as an accompaniment to beans.

4 medium eggplants	**1/2 cup walnuts, chopped**
□	**1/2 cup raisins**
1/3 cup yellow split peas	**1/2 teaspoon dried coriander**
1-1/2 cups water	**1/2 teaspoon dried ginger**
□	**salt and black pepper to taste**
2 tablespoons olive oil	□
1 onion, minced	**wedges of lemon and sprigs of**
1 pound ground turkey	**parsley for garnish**

Cut eggplants in half the long way, leaving stem intact. Place cut side down on an oiled baking sheet. Cover and bake at 375 degrees until tender, about 30-40 minutes.

While eggplant is baking, cover split peas with several inches water in a small pot and cook for 30 minutes, or until they just begin to disintegrate. Drain cooked split peas and set aside.

Gently warm olive oil in a skillet and saute onions until soft, about 5 minutes. Add ground turkey and stir until no pink remains. Add nuts, raisins, coriander and ginger. Add split peas and stir. Season to taste with salt and pepper.

Turn baked eggplant halves over in baking pan. With a fork or spoon mash pulp, taking care not to break the skin. Push aside pulp, making a hollow in each half. Divide filling between eggplants and bake another 15 minutes, until browned on top.

Serve with a wedge of lemon and a sprig of parsley.

SPANISH CHICKEN WITH BLACK OLIVES

Serves 8-10   *Bake at 350*

Inspired by paella, but simpler, with fewer ingredients.

*3 pounds chicken thighs and
   drumsticks*
   ☐
2 tablespoons olive oil
1 onion, diced
6 cloves garlic, minced
1 red bell pepper, diced
3 cups chopped tomatoes
   ☐
*1-6 ounce package Fakin' Bacon,
   diced*

*2 cups raw short-grain
   brown rice*
4 cups boiling water
*pinch saffron (about 3-4
   threads)*
2 teaspoons salt
2 teaspoons black pepper
   ☐
several sprigs fresh parsley
black olives

Preheat oven to 350 degrees.

To make the sauce, gently warm olive oil in a large skillet and
saute onion, garlic, pepper and tomatoes until sauce thickens.
Dice Fakin' Bacon and add to skillet. Saute another 5 minutes,
stirring occasionally.

Spoon sauce into a large shallow baking pan or casserole dish.
Add rice, saffron threads, salt and pepper, and stir until rice is
coated. Pour boiling water into casserole and place chicken
pieces over the top. Bake casserole, uncovered, 45 minutes, or
until rice has absorbed all the liquid and dish is fragrant.

Serve garnished with parsley and olives.

SPICY CHICKEN CURRY

Serves 12

Our favorite, sensual curry sauce. The sauce recipe makes about 6 cups, enough to use and enough to save in a glass jar in the refrigerator for last minute additions to fish, tofu, or beans.

Steamed green beans provide a crunch and color contrast when served as an accompaniment.

Sauce, about 6 cups

1/4 cup olive oil	2 tablespoons lemon juice
8-10 pasilla or poblano whole dried red chiles	2 teaspoons curry powder
8 cloves garlic	2 teaspoons salt
1 large Spanish onion, quartered	4 cups tomato sauce

4 pounds boneless chicken breasts or thighs with the skin removed, cut into bite-sized pieces
8 large steamed potatoes cut into chunks, or 6 cups cooked chickpeas, or 8 cups cooked Basmati rice

a green vegetable, such as string beans.

In a large skillet, gently warm olive oil. Add dried chiles, stirring constantly for 5 minutes. Spoon chiles onto cutting board to cool. Cut stems and tops off and shake out most of the seeds. (Heat is in the seeds, so for a hot sauce, leave more in. Poblano and pasilla chiles are not hot, HOT peppers.)

Using the steel blade of a food processor, blend peppers, garlic and onion, together with lemon juice, curry powder, salt and tomato sauce. Scrape sauce back into skillet with a rubber spatula. Simmer 10 minutes.

continued . . .

SPICY CHICKEN CURRY
(continued)

Leaving 2 cups sauce in skillet, remove 4 cups and refrigerate for future use. Curry sauce keeps for two months under refrigeration.

Add chicken to sauce and simmer over medium heat for 10 minutes. Cover skillet and cook another 30 minutes, or until poultry is thoroughly cooked and has had a chance to absorb the flavors. Add potatoes, chickpeas, or rice to skillet and mix well.

Alternatively, bake chicken and raw potatoes mixed with curry sauce, uncovered in oven until potatoes are soft and chicken is nice and brown, about 1-1/2 to 2 hours.

TURKEY SHEESH KEBABS

Serves 4

These spicy kebabs are excellent served over brown rice or inside pita at a cookout. Or try serving them with black beans and sweet potatoes for contrasting taste and color!

3 cloves garlic, minced
1 medium onion, chopped
1 pound ground turkey
1 pound soft tofu
1 tablespoon whole wheat flour

2 tablespoons lemon juice
2 tablespoons dried parsley
1/2 teaspoon chili powder
1/2 teaspoon black pepper
1/2 teaspoon red pepper
salt to taste, optional

In a bowl combine garlic and onion with ground turkey, tofu, flour, lemon juice, and spices. Use your hands to knead the mixture.

Divide sheesh kebabs into 8 equal long, cigar-shaped burgers.

Broil or grill until lightly browned. Serve hot over rice.

Garnish with a sprig of parsley or watercress.

This makes a great turkey meatloaf. Pat into an ungreased bread pan and bake, uncovered, at 350 degrees for 1 hour.

Seafood Main Dishes

Back at Kallimos . . .

The moonlight glittered on the sea like thousands of restless, fallen stars, and the sand had a blood-red glow from dozens of blazing torches. Men, women, and children, all on their hands and knees, huddled inside the torches' shimmering pools of light. With their bare hands, they were carefully opening freshly turned mounds of sand.

Zachary raced up to us. He took our hands and led us to one of the mounds. As he skipped off to check in with his father, Jude and I knelt down in the still warm sand. Within minutes, we had unearthed a clutch of turtle eggs. We had just transferred them from the nest to our basket when we heard Haleigh behind us. Her voice was filled with alarm. "What," she cried out, "are you doing?"

"We're harvesting the eggs," I answered confidently.

She put her hands on her hips and looked like she was about to explode, but she hesitated for a moment. Then she erupted in laughter. "It is a wonder how you two ever survived before you came here," she declared. "Only a fool would take all the eggs

continued . . .

from a nest. The wise take only one egg from each nest, and always choose the small-est of those they find. The stories say that the turtles have been coming since long before our ancestors became part of this world. Over those long ages, we have come to depend on these eggs as a part of our diet. If we took all of the eggs, or even the best of them, the turtles would stop coming to our shore."

Zachary had returned in time to hear the end of Haleigh's explanation. He chimed in, "The turtles trust us. That's why they come back every year." . . .

Jude and I looked guiltily at our basket and the empty nest in front of us. Without a word, we started putting the eggs back into the nest.

Excerpted from Learning from Hannah © *William H. Thomas, M.D.*

CAJUN SHRIMP JAMBALAYA

Serves 8

Shrimp with a Louisiana beat. Yumm!

1/4 cup olive oil	1 teaspoon thyme
2 onions, chopped	1/2 teaspoon cayenne pepper
4 cloves garlic, minced	1 teaspoon black pepper
1 teaspoon hot pepper flakes	2 cups raw Basmati rice
1 6-oz. package Fakin' Bacon	☐
2 green peppers, diced	1/4 cup dried parsley
☐	☐
3 cups diced tomatoes	salt to taste
☐	☐
3 cups water	2 pounds large shrimp

Gently warm olive oil in a skillet. Saute onions and garlic together with hot pepper flakes, Fakin' Bacon and peppers until onions are soft, about 5 minutes. Add tomatoes and simmer 10 minutes, stirring occasionally.

Add water, thyme, cayenne, black pepper and rice to skillet. Bring jambalaya to a boil. Cover and simmer 40 minutes, or until rice is tender. Stir in parsley. Taste and adjust seasoning.

Add shrimp to skillet, cover and cook 3-5 minutes, until shrimp turn pink.

COLD POACHED FISH WITH AIOLI

Serves 6

An ideal party dish on a warm summer night.

**2 pounds leftover firm, baked
or broiled fish, such as
haddock or tuna
□
1/4 cup fresh lemon juice
1 egg yolk
2 large cloves garlic**

**1/4 teaspoon dried mustard
pinch cayenne pepper
1/2 teaspoon salt
3/4 cup olive or sesame oil
2 tablespoons plain non-fat
yogurt**

This dish assumes one has had the foresight to cook fish ahead. If not, bake or broil fish until translucent and flesh parts easily with a fork.

Using a food processor or blender, blend lemon juice, egg yolk, garlic cloves, mustard, cayenne pepper and salt. With the machine running, slowly pour oil through feed tube. Mix in yogurt.

Aioli is also great on cold vegetables and potatoes.

FISH BAKED WITH PESTO

Serves 6-8   *Bake at 450*

Rich, creamy pesto without nuts accompanies fresh fish. Serve with a grain pilaf and garnish with a sprig of parsley or watercress.

4 scallions, in 1-inch pieces
4 large cloves garlic
1/2 packed cup fresh parsley
1/4 cup fresh basil or tarragon leaves
1-1/2 teaspoons lemon peel

2 tablespoons olive oil
1 teaspoon black pepper
salt to taste
3-4 pounds fish fillets (a firm white fish of your choice)

Preheat oven to 450 degrees.

Using the steel blade of a food processor, blend scallions, garlic, parsley, basil or tarragon, lemon peel, olive oil and black pepper. Stop the machine once or twice to scrape down the sides of the workbowl. Taste pesto and season with salt if desired.

Arrange fish fillets in a baking dish and spread with pesto. Turn fish over and coat second side. Bake uncovered, until tender, about 20 minutes.

GREEK FISH SPETSIOTIKO

Serves 6-8   *Bake at 350*

Fish stew with a mix of tomatoes, olives, garlic and oregano. Typically Greek, typically delicious.

3-4 pounds thick white fish fillets
□
2 tablespoons olive oil
3 large onions, sliced
2 cups diced tomatoes
1/4 cup coarsely chopped olives
1 teaspoon oregano

1 teaspoon black pepper
6 cloves garlic, minced
□
4 hot boiled potatoes, diced
3 tablespoons lemon juice
salt to taste

Preheat oven to 350 degrees.

Gently warm olive oil in a skillet. Saute onion until translucent, about 5 minutes. Add tomatoes, olives, oregano, pepper and garlic. Cover and simmer sauce 5 minutes to give the flavors a chance to blend.

Arrange fish in a baking dish. Add diced potatoes and sauce. Stir and bake, uncovered, until fish flakes easily, about 30 minutes.

When stew is removed from oven, squeeze lemon juice over fish. Taste and adjust seasoning.

HERBED HADDOCK STEW WITH POTATOES

Serves 4

The herbs make a simple stew fragrant and lovely. For a refreshing dessert, serve strawberries with raspberry sauce.

1/4 cup olive oil
2 large onions, chopped
1 clove garlic, minced
1 tomato, diced or 1/4 cup
  tomato sauce
1 green pepper, diced
2 stalks celery, sliced
  ☐
2 bay leaves

1/4 teaspoon each cayenne,
  oregano, basil, thyme
1/2 cup water
4 potatoes, cubed
  ☐
2 pounds haddock fillets, cut
  1-inch thick
  ☐
salt to taste, if desired

Gently warm olive oil in a skillet and saute vegetables. Add herbs, spices, water and cubed potatoes. Cover and simmer 10 minutes, or until mixture is soft and slightly brown.

Place fish on top. Cover and simmer 10 minutes, turn fish and cook another 10. Taste and adjust seasoning.

To serve, place haddock on the side of the plate with the stew beside it.

Substitute halibut, cod, red snapper, or any favorite fish fillet or steak.

HERBED SALMON SAUTEED WITH VEGETABLES

Serves 4

Tender, rosy, juicy salmon steaks with vegetables beneath. Serve with wild or wehani rice.

2 cups water
1 cup wild or wehani rice
□
4 salmon steaks
□
2 carrots, grated
1 stalk celery, sliced
1 large zucchini, sliced
1 large onion, chopped

1 medium tomato, diced
pinch basil, oregano, thyme
and marjoram
4 teaspoons lemon juice
2 teaspoons olive oil
1 teaspoon black pepper
□
lemon wedges for garnish

Bring water to a boil. Stir in rice, cover pot, lower heat and simmer 45 minutes. After 45 minutes, turn off heat and let rice sit in pot, covered, while preparing dish.

Mix vegetables with herbs. Place in a large frying pan or skillet with a cover. Arrange salmon steaks over vegetables. Mix lemon juice and olive oil and pour over fish. Sprinkle with black pepper. Cover pan and simmer 10 minutes.

To serve, place some rice on one-third of the plate, then salmon to the side, garnished with lemon wedges, and vegetables on the remaining third. Salt lightly, if desired.

This yields a light and tender fish and is also suitable for "refreshing" frozen salmon, which might otherwise cook up dry.

MARINATED SOLE WITH PINE NUTS

Serves 6

The delicate flavor and texture of sole combines with wine and the lusciousness of pine nuts.

2 tablespoons olive oil	**□**
4 onions, halved and sliced	**2 tablespoons olive oil**
□	**2 pounds sole fillets**
1/2 cup dry white wine or lemon juice	**□**
1/2 cup cider vinegar	**1/2 cup dry white wine**
1/4 cup pine nuts	**1/2 cup cider vinegar**

Gently warm 2 tablespoons olive oil in a skillet. Saute onions until tender, stirring occasionally, about 5 minutes. Stir in wine, vinegar, and pine nuts. Set aside.

Heat 2 tablespoons olive oil in another skillet. Add sole and saute over medium heat until opaque, 2 minutes per side. Carefully cut sole into bite-sized pieces. Transfer fish to a glass or ceramic pan. Pour the remaining 1/2 cup wine and vinegar over fish. Spoon onion mixture over as well.

Cover and refrigerate 2 days to let the flavors blend.

Bring to room temperature before serving.

MEDITERRANEAN FISH STEW

Serves 4

A classic fish stew with a wonderful blend of basil, oregano, tomato, lemon and saffron. Serve with crusty brown bread or over rice.

1/4 cup olive oil	2 cups diced tomatoes
1 large onion, chopped	2 tablespoons lemon juice or
5 cloves garlic, minced	vinegar
□	□
1 tablespoon dried parsley	1-1/2 pounds cod or haddock,
1 teaspoon basil	cut into chunks
1 teaspoon oregano	1/2 pound scallops
1 teaspoon black pepper	1 cup minced clams with liquid
1/2 teaspoon turmeric	□
pinch saffron	salt to taste

Gently warm olive oil in a large skillet. Add onion and garlic and saute until onion is soft, about 5 minutes. Stir in parsley, basil, oregano, black pepper, turmeric and a pinch of saffron. Add tomatoes and lemon or vinegar and simmer 5 minutes.

Stir in fish, scallops, and clams with liquid and simmer until fish is tender, about 20 minutes.

Taste and add salt if desired.

RUSSIAN FISH CAKES

Serves 6

Succulent fish cakes with a crispy coating. Accompany with cucumber rounds or coleslaw. Garnish with a sprig of fresh dill.

2 tablespoons olive oil
2 onions, finely chopped
☐
3 slices wholegrain bread
☐
1-1/2 pound haddock, cod, or halibut cut into 2-inch pieces
1 large carrot, grated
1 teaspoon dried dill weed
3 tablespoons lemon juice

1 tablespoon black pepper
salt to taste
☐
1/4 cup plain no-fat yogurt
1/4 cup mayonnaise or Nayonaise
1 teaspoon dried dill weed
☐
3 tablespoons olive oil
1 cup soy granules or grits
sprigs of dill to garnish

Gently warm olive oil in a medium skillet. Add onions and saute until golden, 10 minutes. Transfer to a large bowl.

Using the steel blade of a food processor, process bread in food processor into crumbs. Process fish with on/off turns until ground, but not pureed. Transfer to bowl. Use the grating disk to grate carrot or grate by hand. Add carrot together with dill, lemon and pepper to fish. Knead well to blend. Cover and refrigerate 1 hour to firm fish.

Mix yogurt, mayonnaise or Nayonaise and dill. Set aside.

Form fish into 3-inch oval patties. Heat oil in a large, heavy skillet. Coat patties in soy granules. Saute fish cakes over medium heat until golden, about 4 minutes per side. Serve with a dollop of yogurt sauce and garnish with a sprig of dill.

SCALLOP SAUTE WITH CHINESE VEGETABLES

Serves 8-10

Savory and slightly sweet, garnish with toasted soynuts or cashews.

2 pounds scallops	2 4-oz. cans sliced water
1/4 cup tamari soy sauce	chestnuts
1/4 cup olive or sesame oil	2 4-oz. cans bamboo shoots
4 cloves garlic, minced	1 pound snow peas, stringed
1 teaspoon black pepper	a handful of dulse (mild tasting,
□	salty seaweed)
1 cup toasted soynuts or	2 cups mushrooms, thickly
cashews for garnish	sliced

Marinate scallops for two hours, or up to 24, in tamari, oil, garlic and black pepper.

If using cashews, toast on a cookie sheet in a 250 degree oven for 15 minutes. Set aside to cool.

Heat a wok or large skillet and stir-fry scallops in marinade until opaque, about 3 minutes. Add vegetables and stir-fry just until snow peas have turned bright green and dulse has turned red, about 2 minutes.

Serve immediately over rice noodles or hot rice. Garnish with soynuts or cashews.

SHRIMP AND FISH CASSEROLE WITH ROMANO

Serves 6

Three favorite foods, shrimp, fish and Pecorino Romano cheese, give this dish a festive air. Serve over pasta or rice.

2 tablespoons olive oil
1 onion, chopped
3 cloves garlic, minced
☐
1 15-ounce can tomatoes
3/4 teaspoon oregano
1 teaspoon black pepper
☐

2 pounds cod, scrod, haddock,
  or halibut, in 3/4 inch pieces
1/4 pound medium raw shrimp,
  peeled and deveined
☐
3/4 cup grated Pecorino
  Romano cheese
parsley for garnish

Gently warm olive oil in a large skillet. Saute onion and garlic until soft, about 5 minutes.

Stir in tomatoes, oregano and pepper. Bring to a boil. Reduce heat, cover and simmer 10 minutes, stirring occasionally.

Add fish to skillet and stir to coat. Cover and simmer 10 minutes. Add shrimp and cook, uncovered, just until shrimp turn pink, about 5 minutes.

Serve at once over pasta and sprinkle with Romano. Garnish with parsley.

SHRIMP CURRY WITH POTATOES

Serves 8

Accompany with steamed asparagus or spinach. Or make with 2 pounds tofu instead of shrimp. In this case, you may want to increase the amount of spices.

8 medium red potatoes, scrubbed, unpeeled and cut into quarters
□
4 tablespoons olive oil
4 onions, chopped
1 teaspoon salt
1 teaspoon ground coriander

1 teaspoon curry
1 1-pound can Italian peeled tomatoes, drained
2 pounds peeled and deveined shrimp
□
1 lemon
watercress for garnish

Steam or bake potatoes until tender when pierced by a fork. Set aside.

Gently warm olive oil in a skillet. Saute onions until tender, about 5 minutes. Add spices and stir over low heat 5 minutes. Add tomatoes, shrimp and cooked potatoes. Simmer just until tomatoes are hot and shrimp have turned pink, another 5 minutes. Squeeze juice of lemon over entire dish.

Garnish with watercress and serve at once.

SOLE WITH BUTTER AND ALMONDS

Serves 4

Deliciously decadent - almonds browned in butter spooned over sole. Equally luscious and rich olive oil can be used in place of butter.

4 sole fillets, about 1-1/2 pounds	**1/4 cup dry white wine**
❑	**2 tablespoons fresh lemon juice**
6 tablespoons butter	❑
1/2 cup almonds	**lemon wedges, for garnish**

Melt butter in a large skillet over medium high heat. Add almonds and cook until heated through, about 1 minute.

Add wine and lemon juice to skillet. Simmer until sauce is slightly thickened, stirring constantly.

Broil sole 2 minutes. Turn and pour sauce over fish and broil for another 2 minutes.

Serve garnished with lemon wedges. Accompany with boiled rice.

THAI-SCENTED SHRIMP KEBABS

Serves 6-8

The key to making delicious kebabs is in the long marination. So marinate this the night before.

14 ounces unsweetened coconut milk
1/2 cup lemon or lime juice
2 tablespoons minced ginger
2 cloves garlic, minced
3 tablespoons soy sauce
1 tablespoon rice syrup
1 teaspoon dried lemon grass
1 tablespoon sesame or olive oil
1/2 teaspoon salt
1/2 teaspoon crushed red pepper

2 pounds large shrimp, peeled and deveined
2 red bell peppers, cut into 24 triangles
□
1 tablespoon black sesame seeds
1/2 cup chopped parsley

In a small pan, whisk coconut milk with lemon or lime juice, ginger, garlic, soy sauce, rice syrup, lemon grass, oil, salt and crushed red pepper. Bring to a boil over moderately high heat and boil 1 minute. Set aside to cool.

Pour cooled marinade over shrimp. Refrigerate covered, for at least 12 hours and up to 24.

Preheat a broiler. Mix shrimp with peppers and broil in marinade, turning once, until shrimp are cooked through and the peppers charred, about 5 minutes. Transfer to a platter and sprinkle with sesame seeds and chopped parsley.

Serve with black or red Thai rice.

Desserts

Back at Kallimos . . .

"Tell me, child, what did you learn?"

I drew a deep breath. "Before that story, I did not understand the relationship between patience and courage. In the Other World, courage is found in dramatic gestures and acts of bravery. The courage to be patient is something we rarely think of as courage. Now I can see that patient courage is the true courage. I've always wanted the next

continued . . .

thing in my life to come to me <u>now</u>. I remember being a child and seeing my sister break out with pimples on her face. I wanted to have pimples on my face right then and there. I didn't want to wait. But, when they did come to me, I wanted them to go away."

Haleigh gazed into the fire and nodded. "When we left for Shah-Pan, you wanted to be in Shah-Pan. When we arrived, you would, no doubt, want to be home in the village."

"For a long time—my whole life, I guess—I've been living in a cage. I've been a prisoner to what comes next. You are trying to set me free, aren't you?"

"Yes, I would love to see you live the way a human being was meant to live."

Brimming with enthusiasm, I asked, "When can I start?"

Haleigh let out a rasping chuckle that escalated into a laugh. "My dear child, you begin right now, right here, in this moment. The only moment you will ever know, the present."

Excerpted from Learning from Hannah © *William H. Thomas, M.D.*

ALMOND CRUST ICE CREAM PIE

Serves 8-10

Substitute toasted pecans or macadamia nuts for almonds. Use any dense, good quality ice cream. Non-dairy works too. Try swirling two flavors together in the pie plate with a butter knife.

1-1/2 cups almonds, coarsely chopped
2-3 pints dense vanilla ice cream or
   non-dairy "ice cream"

berries, peaches,
   apricots
mint leaves, for garnish

Toast chopped almonds on a cookie sheet for 10 minutes at 350 degrees. Remove and cool completely.

Soften ice cream in refrigerator until spreadable.

Distribute 1 cup chopped almonds evenly in pie plate. Spoon softened ice cream over almonds. Compress and smooth using a rubber spatula.

Sprinkle remaining almonds over pie. Cover with plastic wrap and freeze two hours before serving. Ice cream pie may be prepared ahead and frozen for up to 1 week.

When ready to serve, soften pie in refrigerator 20 minutes. Serve in small wedges garnished with a few perfect berries, or slices of peach or apricot and add a few mint leaves.

APPLE BROWN BETTY

Serves 6   *Bake at 325*

Apple brown betty makes a great breakfast, too, with a mug of steaming herbal tea, a glass of milk or soy milk. May be served with whipped cream, or a la mode.

8-10 apples, peeled and sliced
1/2 cup all-fruit strawberry or
**   raspberry jam or jelly**
☐
1 cup nuts or seeds

1 cup oats or other grain flakes
**   such as spelt, triticale**
2 tablespoons fruit concentrate
2 teaspoons cinnamon

Preheat oven to 325 degrees.

Combine apples with jam. Place in a 12 x 8-inch baking pan, pyrex dish, or deep pie plate.

Using the steel blade of a food processor, whirl nuts, oats, fruit concentrate, and cinnamon with quick on/off turns until mixture resembles coarse meal.

Crumble topping evenly over apples and place pan in the oven. Bake 30-45 minutes, or until topping is nicely browned and apples are soft and bubbly.

Serve warm or cold.

Our favorite apples to use with this are the tart ones. MacIntosh or Granny Smiths work well, too.

APRICOT SPICE CAKE WITH WALNUTS

Serves 12-14   *Bake at 350*

Moist and wonderful. Keeps well and serves many.

1-1/2 cups dried apricots	2 cups w/w pastry flour
1-1/2 cups water	2 teaspoons cinnamon
☐	2 teaspoons allspice
1 cup canola or safflower oil	1 teaspoon nutmeg
1 cup rice syrup or barley malt	1/2 teaspoon salt
1 cup fruit concentrate or honey	1 teaspoon baking soda
1 tablespoon vanilla extract	☐
3 eggs	2 cups walnuts, chopped
1 cup sour milk or yogurt	

Simmer apricots in water until soft. Puree in blender or food processor, adding a tablespoon more water if necessary.

Preheat oven to 350 degrees.

Grease a 10-inch tube pan.

With an electric mixer, on low-medium speed, beat together oil, sweeteners, vanilla, eggs, sour milk or yogurt, and apricot puree.

Mix in dry ingredients using low speed. Then incorporate walnuts.

Pour batter into pan and bake 45 minutes, or until a knife inserted in the center of the cake comes out clean. Remove cake from oven and let cool for 15 minutes in the pan on a rack. Remove cake from the pan to finish cooling on rack.

BAVARIAN WHIPPED CREAM

Serves 6

A snap to prepare! Elegant served in wine goblets. Substitute vanilla yogurt for whipping cream for a low-calorie version.

1 cup heavy whipping cream
2 tablespoons honey or fruit
concentrate
1 teaspoon vanilla extract

2 cups fresh berries, peaches
apricots, pitted cherries
or blueberries

perfect berries or fruit for
garnish

Using an electric mixer, whip cream until stiff peaks form. Gradually beat in honey and vanilla.

Fold fruit into whipped cream with a rubber spatula. Spoon into goblets or dessert bowls. Cover and chill thoroughly before serving. Garnish with perfect berries or slices of whole fruit.

BIRDSEED CLUSTERS

Makes 16

Similar to sesame spice candies, birdseed clusters have a different charm and are, perhaps, easier to make because they don't have to be cut or patted out.

1 cup sunflower seeds   **1/2 cup barley malt**
1 cup pumpkin seeds   **1/2 teaspoon cinnamon**
        ☐   **1/4 teaspoon ginger**
1/4 cup honey

Grease two 12x12 shallow baking pans or cookie sheets.

Follow the directions for making Sesame Spice Candy.

Instead of spooning batter into prepared pans and patting out, use a 1/4 cup measure or large soup spoon and dollop out clumps of hot mixture onto pans. When batter is distributed, use the heel of your hand to flatten clusters. Don't press too hard as candy may still be hot and can burn.

Cool 10 minutes and then remove clusters with a metal spatula. Place on serving plate in a single layer so candies don't melt into one another.

Candies may be frozen on cookie sheets for a few minutes before removing with a metal spatula. Then stack and store in the freezer. When frozen, candies are brittle, so don't drop!

BLUEBERRY PIE

Serves 6   *Bake at 350*

Our adaptation of a favorite from the Deaf Smith Country
Cookbook. Adding thyme makes cultivated blueberries taste like
wild ones.

1 unbaked 9-inch whole wheat	**1 tablespoon lemon juice**
pie crust	**1/2 teaspoon nutmeg**
6 cups fresh or frozen blueberries	**2 tablespoons arrowroot**
4 tablespoons whole wheat flour	**pinch sea salt**
1/2 cup pure maple syrup	**pinch thyme**

Preheat oven to 350 degrees.

Mix berries with the remaining ingredients and spoon into
crust. Let stand 15 minutes.

Place pie on a cookie sheet to make carrying to the oven
easier and to catch blueberry drips while pie bakes!

Bake 1-1/2 hours, or until crust begins to brown and
blueberries begin to firm. (Pie will solidify somewhat as it
cools.)

Remove cookie sheet from oven and cool pie on a wire rack.
Serve blueberry pie warm, room temperature, or cold.

Substitute pitted cherries or sliced peaches for blueberries.

CAROB CAKE

Serves 8   *Bake at 325*

Rich, dark, wonderful. May be served with whipped cream.

1/2 cup carob powder
3/4 cup boiling water
□

1-1/2 cups w/w pastry flour
1-1/2 teaspoons baking powder
1 teaspoon cinnamon
1 teaspoon salt

□
1 cup honey
1/2 cup safflower oil
8 eggs, separated
□
3 teaspoons vanilla

Preheat oven to 325 degrees. Whisk together carob powder and boiling water in small bowl until no lumps remain.

In a small bowl, combine flour, baking powder, cinnamon and salt.

Using an electric mixer, cream honey with oil on medium speed. Add yolks, one at a time. Blend in cooled carob mixture and vanilla. Add dry ingredients and beat until batter is smooth.

Beat whites in a clean bowl with clean beater on high speed. Remove bowl from mixer, pour carob batter over whites, and fold in quickly and gently using a wire whisk. Do not over blend.

Turn cake into ungreased 10-inch tube pan. Bake 1 hour. Remove pan from oven to stand 5-10 minutes on a wire rack and then invert to cool. When cool, remove cake from pan by running a knife around the edges to loosen.

CAROB CONFECTIONS

Makes approx 42 balls

No-bake, fudge-like confections. Glossy and chocolaty.

1 cup honey	1 cup sesame seeds
1 cup unsalted, crunchy	1/2 cup wheat germ
peanut butter	1/2 cup soy granules
☐	1 teaspoon cinnamon
1 cup carob powder	1 teaspoon almond extract
1 cup sunflower seeds	

Beat honey and peanut butter together until "liquidy," using a wooden spoon.

Only then, mix in dry ingredients and extract. Again, use a wooden spoon or knead with your hands. Dough will be sticky, stiff and hard to mix. Persevere!

Pinch off pieces of dough about the size of walnuts and roll between your hands until smooth and shiny.

Store confections in the refrigerator, but bring to room temperature before eating.

CAROB MOUSSE CAKE

Serves 12   *Bake at 325*

Mousse cake, custardy and soft. For a festive look, pipe whipped cream on top and garnish with toasted almond pieces.

1-1/4 cups ground almonds	**1 teaspoon vanilla**
☐	**1/2 cup whole wheat pastry**
1 pound barley-malt sweetened	**flour**
carob block, broken into pieces,	**1/4 cup honey**
or carob chips or disks	☐
1 cup whipping cream	**whipped cream**
☐	**toasted almonds**
6 eggs	

Preheat oven to 325 degrees. Grease a 9-inch springform pan. Press almonds onto bottom and 1-1/2 inches up sides.

Using the steel blade of a food processor, chop carob block. If using carob chips or disks, no chopping is necessary. In a small pot, bring whipping cream to a boil. With the food processor running, pour hot cream through the feedtube and blend until mixture is smooth.

Using an an electric mixer on low speed, beat eggs and vanilla for 2 minutes. Add flour and honey; beat on high for 10 minutes, or until batter is thick and lemon colored. Gradually add carob mixture into batter. Turn into prepared pan and bake 45 minutes, or until puffed on the outer third of top. Center will be slightly soft. Do not overbake; remember, cake should have the consistency of custard.

Do not remove cake from pan. Cool 3-4 hours or overnight. To serve, run knife around outside of cake and carefully remove sides of springform pan.

CARROT APPLESAUCE CAKE WITH APRICOT GLAZE

Serves 10   *Bake at 350*

Another old-fashioned favorite with an update - no cream cheese frosting but a beautiful golden apricot glaze.

2 cups w/w pastry flour	**1-1/4 cup honey or fruit**
1 cup oats	**concentrate**
1 1/2 teaspoons baking powder	**1 teaspoon vanilla**
1 1/2 teaspoons baking soda	**1-2/3 cups applesauce**
1 tablespoon cinnamon	**1 pound grated carrots**
1 teaspoon nutmeg	**4 eggs**
1 teaspoon salt	**3/4 cup canola or safflower oil**
❑	❑
1 cup raisins	**1 cup all-fruit apricot jam**

Preheat oven to 350 degrees.   Grease two 9-inch cake pans.

Mix the dry ingredients together. Mix wet and add to dry. Stir just until moistened.

Spoon batter into prepared pans and bake 60 minutes, or until knife inserted in the center comes out clean and cake pulls away from the sides of the pan.

Remove cakes from oven and place pans on cooling racks for 20 minutes. Remove cakes from pans to finish cooling on rack.

Place one cake layer, flat side up, on cake plate. Smear a thin layer of apricot jam over cake. Place second layer, rounded side up, on top of first layer. Spread with remainder of apricot jam, sealing top and sides. Decorate with pieces of apricot from jam.

FRUIT COMPOTE WITH BERRIES

Serves 12

Inspired by Grandma Ida. A variation on an old favorite, stewed fruit compote. The colors are rich and beautiful.

1 cup pitted prunes	**1 cinnamon stick**
1 cup dried apricots	☐
1 cup dried peaches	**1 cup fresh blueberries**
1/4 cup dried pineapple	**1 cup fresh strawberries**
6 cups water	**1 ripe banana**

In a large, heavy pot, combine prunes, apricots, peaches, and pineapple with water and cinnamon stick. Bring to a simmer. Turn off heat and cool compote.

Refrigerate overnight to let flavors ripen.

Thirty minutes before serving, spoon 1 cup compote per person in large bowl. Add berries. Slice in banana. Stir gently so as not to crush berries. Chill for 30 minutes and serve in dessert bowls.

Compote can be served without fresh fruit, useful in winter.

HONEY WHOLE WHEAT SPONGE CAKE

Serves 6   *Bake at 300*

Delicious served with fresh berries, even for breakfast!

6 eggs, separated   **2 teaspoons vanilla**
1 cup honey   **1-1/2 cups w/w pastry flour**
1/2 teaspoon salt

Preheat oven to 300 degrees.

Using an electric mixer, beat egg whites at the highest speed until soft peaks form. While still beating, drizzle in 1/2 cup honey and salt. Continue to beat until stiff peaks form, or until mixture clings to bowl.

In a second bowl, beat yolks with the same beaters, gradually adding the remaining honey and vanilla, until thick and light in color.

Using a wire whisk or a rubber spatula, fold yolk mixture into whites, gently, but quickly. Fold in flour. Turn batter into an ungreased nine-inch tube cake pan and bake one hour.

Remove cake pan from oven and invert to cool cake. When completely cool, loosen cake with a butter knife by running knife around the sides of the pan and the tube. Turn pan over onto hand and gently remove cake to a cake plate.

INDIAN PUDDING

Serves 12   *Bake at 350*

Indian pudding is one of the most traditional of Colonial desserts. We think our version is one of the best!

1-1/2 cups cornmeal
8 cups lo-fat milk
☐
2 tablespoons butter
1/4 cup molasses
1/3 cup honey
1/2 cup maple syrup

1/4 teaspoon salt
1/2 teaspoon ginger
1-1/2 teaspoons cinnamon
☐
3 eggs, beaten
1 cup raisins

Preheat oven to 350 degrees.

Combine cornmeal and 3 cups milk in a saucepan and stir with a wire whisk until smooth. Add the remaining milk and cook over medium heat, whisking, until it thickens and mixture comes to a boil. Simmer 2 minutes. Remove from heat, stir in butter, sweetening and spices.

Whisk a little of the hot mixture into the eggs. Slowly add egg mixture back into hot cornmeal, stirring to prevent eggs from cooking. Stir in raisins.

Grease an 11x14 inch baking pan. Pour pudding into pan and bake one hour, or until set around edges and browned. Indian Pudding will continue to cook when removed from the oven, so it should not be completely set when you take it out.

Serve warm or at room temperature. Chill leftovers.

OLD-FASHIONED PECAN PIE

Serves 6   *Bake at 350*

New England farm cooks of old used maple syrup in large amounts. Here, maple syrup is "cut" with the addition of barley malt and carob, which gives the pie a luscious, thick richness without butter.

1 unbaked 9-inch w/w pie crust	*1 tablespoon whole wheat flour*
☐	*1 tablespoon carob powder*
1 cup maple syrup	*1/4 teaspoon salt*
1/2 cup barley malt syrup	*1/2 teaspoon nutmeg*
4 eggs, beaten	☐
	1 cup pecans

Using an electric mixer, food processor, or a wooden spoon, beat all ingredients, except the pecans, together. Stir in pecans and pour pie filling into crust.

Place pie plate on cookie sheet to bake in oven for 1 hour at 350 degrees, or until pie is slightly firm to touch and nicely browned. The cookie sheet will catch the drips and make cleanup easier.

The pecans will rise to top of pie as it bakes. When the pie is baked, remove from the oven and cool on a rack.

ORANGE SEED STRIPS

Makes 18 large cookies   *Bake at 300*

My version of a favorite from Brownies Restaurant in New York City, an institution which is, sadly, no more.

1/4 cup powdered milk	2 teaspoons vanilla
2-1/2 cups w/w pastry flour	1 teaspoon orange extract
1/2 cup soy flour	1 tablespoon water
1/2 teaspoon cinnamon	☐
1 cup raw sugar or Sucanat	1/2 cup sunflower seeds
1/2 cup safflower oil	1/2 cup brown sesame seeds
2 eggs (reserve 1 white)	sesame seeds for sprinkling

Preheat oven to 300 degrees.   Grease two cookie sheets.

Mix all ingredients except sunflower and sesame seeds using the steel blade of a food processor and on/off turns until the batter moves freely under the blade. Knead dough by running machine for another minute, stopping once or twice to scrape down sides of the workbowl with a rubber spatula.

Add sunflower and sesame seeds. Quickly turn machine on/off several times to incorporate seeds.

Divide dough into 4 balls and roll each into a 9-inch rope. Place on cookie sheets and flatten 4 inches wide. Brush each with reserved egg white mixed with 1-2 tablespoons water. Sprinkle cookies with sesame seeds.

Bake 30 minutes, or until nicely browned and aromatic. Remove from oven and cut into 2-inch strips.

PECAN CRUST CHEESECAKE WITH FRESH PEACHES

Serves 12   *Bake at 300*

Crust
- 1/2 cup toasted wheat germ
- 1/2 cup pecans
- 1/2 teaspoon cinnamon

Topping
- 2 cups fresh peaches,
    peeled and sliced
- 1/4 cup all-fruit
    strawberry jam

Filling
- 2 pounds cottage cheese
- 8 ounces cream cheese
- 3/4 cup honey
- 2 teaspoons vanilla
- 1/4 cup w/w pastry flour
- 6 large eggs

Preheat oven to 300 degrees.

Toast pecans on a cookie sheet for 15 minutes. Remove from oven and cool completely.

Butter a 9-inch springform pan.

Using the steel blade of a food processor, grind pecans, wheat germ and cinnamon. Turn into pan and gently shake to distribute.

Place filling ingredients in workbowl. Blend filling until smooth and no pieces of cream cheese remain. Stop the machine once or twice to scrape down sides of workbowl with a rubber spatula. Gently pour cheese batter over crust. (Some crust will rise at first.) Place cake in oven and bake 1 hour. Turn off heat, but leave oven door closed another 1-1/2 hours. Then, remove cake and cool completely before covering and storing overnight in the refrigerator.

continued . . .

PECAN CRUST CHEESECAKE WITH FRESH PEACHES
(continued)

To serve, run a knife around the sides of the pan and carefully open springform to remove cake to a serving plate.

In a small pot, melt jam and add sliced peaches. Toss gently. Place peaches in a decorative pattern on top of the cheesecake and serve.

Instead of peaches, try strawberries, kiwi, blueberries, or fresh apricots. Combine fruits to make a colorful design.

Cheesecake without fruit can be refrigerated 2-3 days. With a fruit topping, cheesecake should be served immediately.

PLUM AND BLUEBERRY CRISP

Serves 6-8   *Bake at 325, 350*

If you prefer your crisp warm, not to worry. Make ahead, if desired, and set aside. When ready for dessert, reheat at 350 degrees for 10 minutes.

Topping
- *1/3 cup pecans, chopped*
- ☐
- *1 cup w/w pastry flour*
- *1/2 cup rolled oats*
- *1/2 cup honey or fruit*
  concentrate

Fruit Filling
- *3 cups prune plums,*
  pitted and sliced
- *3 cups blueberries*
- *1/4 cup honey or fruit*
  concentrate
- *1 tablespoon arrowroot*
- *1 teaspoon nutmeg*

Preheat oven to 325 degrees. Spread pecans on a cookie sheet and toast in oven until lightly browned, about 5-8 minutes.

Increase oven temperature to 350 degrees.

In a bowl, toss plums with blueberries, sweetener, arrowroot and nutmeg. Spoon into a 2-1/2 quart deep baking dish.

In another bowl, blend chopped toasted pecans, flour, oats, and honey or fruit concentrate until the mixture resembles a streusel topping.

Crumble the topping evenly over fruit. Place baking dish on a cookie sheet in the oven and bake 45 minutes, or until fruit juice begins to bubble and top is lightly browned. (The cookie sheet will catch any drips and make cleanup easier.) Remove crisp from oven and cool on a rack. Serve warm.

POPPY SEED CHEESECAKE

Serves 12   *Bake at 350*

For poppy seed lovers, a beautiful cheesecake!

Filling
- **1 pound cream cheese, cut into pieces**
- **1 pound cottage cheese**
- **4 eggs**
- **1/2 cup honey**
- **1 tablespoon orange juice**
- **1 teaspoon vanilla extract**

Topping I
- **1 cup dark raisins**
- **1/2 cup water**
- **1-1/2 cups poppy seeds**
- **1/2 cup milk**
- **1/2 cup honey**
- **1 teaspoon vanilla extract**

Topping II
- **1/2 cup walnuts**
- **1/2 cup w/w pastry flour**
- **1 teaspoon cinnamon**
- **2 tablespoons butter**
- **1/4 cup honey**

Preheat oven to 350 degrees.

Filling

Using the steel blade of a food processor, blend the filling until no lumps of cream cheese remain. Stop machine once or twice to scrape down the sides of the workbowl with a rubber spatula.

Pour cheese mixture into the springform pan and bake one hour. Remove cheesecake from oven. Allow to cool in pan on a rack while toppings are prepared.

continued . . .

POPPY SEED CHEESECAKE
(continued)

Topping I

Chop raisins using the steel blade and place in a saucepan with water. Cook over medium heat until water has evaporated.

Crush poppy seeds in an electric coffee grinder or blender until they resemble a dark gray powder. Add poppyseeds, milk, and honey to raisins. Simmer 15 minutes, stirring, to prevent from sticking or burning. Topping will become quite thick.

Remove and cool. Stir in vanilla.

Spread poppy seed topping over cheesecake. Do not remove cake from the springform pan.

Topping II

Using the steel blade, coarsely chop walnuts together with flour and cinnamon by turning machine on and off 3 times. Push butter into walnuts and drizzle honey on top. Turn the machine on/off several times, until no pieces of butter remain and the mixture is a streusel topping. Crumble over poppy seed mixture.

Slide cake under the broiler and broil just until top browns - 1 or 2 minutes. Watch cake CAREFULLY because it browns QUICKLY!

Refrigerate cheesecake overnight in the springform pan. To serve, run knife around edges, carefully open springform and remove cake to a serving plate.

PORTUGUESE MAPLE FLAN

Serves 10   *Bake at 300*

A rich maple custard - the ultimate creamy dessert.

1 cup maple syrup   **4 eggs, room temperature**
□   **1 teaspoon vanilla extract**
3 cups half-and-half

Preheat oven to 300 degrees. In a small saucepan, bring 3/4 cup maple syrup to a boil over moderate heat. Boil, stirring occasionally, for 10 minutes. Remove pan from stove and stir briefly so foam subsides. Pour into a 6-cup ring mold (or use an oven-proof dish); tilt quickly to evenly coat bottom of mold.

In the same saucepan, bring half-and-half to a boil over moderate heat, stirring to dissolve remaining syrup.

Meanwhile, beat eggs with an electric mixer until thick. Drizzle in remaining 1/4 cup maple syrup. With mixer still running, gradually pour hot cream into beaten eggs. Stir in vanilla. Strain through a mesh strainer or cheesecloth into mold. Place mold in a larger pan, and place pan in the oven. Add enough hot water to reach halfway up the mold.

Bake 1 hour, or longer (sometimes as much as another 45 minutes, depending upon mold, weather, etc.) until custard is set and a knife inserted in the center comes out clean. Remove mold from water bath and cool. Refrigerate 3 hours or overnight.

To serve, run knife around the edge and invert flan onto a serving plate with a lip so syrup will not run on floor! Hit bottom of pan smartly with palm of your hand. Flan should come out. If not, repeat procedure.

POT DE CREME CAROB

Serves 6

A lovely and rich carob mousse. Even those who profess to hate carob have been known to lick the bowl.

3/4 pound malt-sweetened carob block in 1/2-inch pieces or carob disks or chips

2 cups heavy cream
6 egg yolks
1-1/2 teaspoons vanilla

Using the steel blade of a food processor, chop carob bar with on/off turns. If using chips or disks, no chopping is necessary. Place them in the workbowl of the processor.

Bring cream to a boil. With the processor motor running, slowly pour cream through feed tube. Whirl until smooth, about 30 seconds. Add egg yolks one at a time. Blend 10 seconds after each. Add vanilla.

Pour pot de creme carob into six pot de creme pots or pretty liqueur glasses. Cover each. Refrigerate for several hours or overnight before serving.

Serve plain or with a dollop of whipped cream. To speed up serving time, freeze for 2 hours. Soften slightly in refrigerator before serving.

Save egg whites in a glass jar in the refrigerator to use in meringues for Baked Alaska or macaroons.

SESAME SPICE CANDY

Makes 48

Old-world candies redolent with cinnamon and ginger.

Don't make on a rainy day as honey absorbs moisture and candies will be sticky. If sticky, candy may be frozen until ready to eat.

2 cups brown sesame seeds	**1/2 cup barley malt**
☐	**1/2 teaspoon cinnamon**
1/4 cup honey	**1/4 teaspoon ginger**

Grease a 12x12 shallow baking pan.

Toast sesame seeds in an ungreased skillet, stirring over medium-high heat 5-10 minutes until aromatic and seeds begin to pop. Transfer to a bowl, making sure that there are no seeds left in the skillet.

Put honey, barley malt, cinnamon and ginger in skillet and bring to a full rolling boil over low heat, stirring often. Cook syrup 4 minutes. Remove skillet from heat and quickly stir in sesame seeds. Quickly turn hot mixture into prepared pan. Using a light touch, pat out with rubber spatula and then the palm of your hand. A heavy touch will cause hot candy to stick. If necessary, wet hands with cold water to pat. Do this sparingly, so honey won't have much water to absorb.

Cool candy 10 minutes, then test to see if cool enough to cut into squares and squares into triangles. Don't wait too long to cut or candy will harden. Once cut, cool completely before storing in an airtight container.

STRAWBERRIES WITH RASPBERRY SAUCE

Serves 4-6

Wonderful with a hint of almond flavoring!

10 ounces fresh/frozen raspberries
2 tablespoons honey or fruit
   concentrate
1 tablespoon lemon juice
   ☐
1 quart fresh strawberries
2 tablespoons honey or fruit juice
   concentrate

1/2 teaspoon almond extract
   ☐
slivered almonds, optional
vanilla ice cream, optional
whipped cream, optional

For sauce: Using the steel blade of a food processor or a blender, puree raspberries. Strain to remove seeds. Place in pot with sweetener and lemon juice. Bring to a slow boil and cook over low heat 2 minutes. Cool sauce and set aside.

Wash and hull strawberries. Gently toss strawberries with sweetener and almond extract. Pour cooled raspberry sauce over berries and chill, covered, for several hours before serving. Garnish with toasted, slivered almonds, or a dollop of ice cream or whipped cream.

Sliced fresh peaches or apricots may be substituted for strawberries.

STRAWBERRY APRICOT TARTLETS

Makes 12 tartletts   *Bake at 400*

Individual tartlets are pretty and elegant to serve. Dried apricots and fresh strawberries make a mouth-watering combination.

Crust

2-1/2 cups w/w pastry flour	**1/4 teaspoon salt**
1/2 cup ground almonds	**1/2 cup canola oil**
1/4 teaspoon cinnamon	**1/3 cup honey or fruit concentrate**

Preheat oven to 400 degrees.

In a bowl, blend together crust ingredients, which should hold together when a clump is pressed between fingers. If crust seems too dry, add a spoonful of water; if too wet, add a spoonful of flour. Grease 12 tartlet shells with removable bottoms. Divide and press dough into shells. Prick with a fork. Bake 15 minutes.

Remove tartlets from oven and cool completely before pressing bottom of forms up gently to unmold shells.

Filling

1-1/2 cups dried apricots, snipped coarsely	**4 teaspoons arrowroot**
1/2 cup apricot juice, or mango or strawberry	□
	1 pint strawberries
	2 tablespoons all-fruit jam

Place apricots in juice with arrowroot. Bring to a boil over low heat. Stir and turn off heat. Allow apricot mixture to cool.

Divide apricot mixture between shells, place fresh berries on top and brush with melted jam.

SWEET POTATO PIE

Serves 6   *Bake at 450, 350*

Dedicated to Andrea Morgan, one of our original crew who was delighted not to have to peel pumpkin. Unusually wholesome and delicious - great even for breakfast! A pound of tofu can be substituted for the eggs and milk.

1 unbaked 9-inch w/w pie crust	**2 teaspoons vanilla extract**
☐	**1 teaspoon cinnamon**
3 pounds (about 3-1/2 cups)	**1/2 teaspoon ground cloves**
sweet potatoes, boiled soft	**1/2 teaspoon allspice**
1 cup milk or soy milk	**1/4 teaspoon nutmeg**
3 eggs, beaten	**1/4 teaspoon ginger**
1/2 cup maple syrup	**1/4 teaspoon salt**

Preheat oven to 450 degrees.

Using the steel blade of a food processor, blend sweet potatoes (don't peel) together with remaining ingredients until the batter is smooth and flows easily under the blade.

Pour mixture into unbaked crust. Place pie in oven and bake at 450 degrees for 10 minutes, then reduce oven temperature to 350 degrees and bake an additional 45 minutes, or until pie is set.

Take pie out of oven and set on a rack. Cool before cutting. Serve plain or with a whipped topping.

TAHINI KEENIES

Makes 36 cookies   *Bake at 350*

Tahini, or sesame butter, rich in calcium and minerals, is an excellent source of protein.   Tahini Keenies are a meal in themselves.

1-1/2 cups tahini   **2 teaspoons cinnamon**
2 cups honey   **6-8 cups rolled oats**

Beat together tahini and honey in a large bowl with a heavy wooden spoon until "liquidy" and creamy. Blend in cinnamon and oats. (This mixture will be quite sticky!)

Grease cookie sheets and preheat oven to 350 degrees.

Drop dough by tablespoonfuls onto cookie sheets. Flatten slightly with palm of hands. If batter sticks to your hands, wet them.

Bake cookies for 20-25 minutes, or until lightly golden. Place cookie sheet on wire racks to cool for 5-10 minutes. When cool, remove cookies with a metal spatula to cool completely on racks.

WALNUT SURPRISE COOKIES

Makes 16 squares   *Bake at 350*

Walnut surprise cookies have sentimental value - the first cookie my brothers and I learned to make. Impossible to eat just one!

1 cup turbinado sugar or Sucanat	1/2 cup w/w pastry flour
1 egg	1/4 teaspoon salt
1 teaspoon vanilla	1 cup walnuts, chopped
☐	1/2 cup carob chips

Preheat oven to 350 degrees.   Grease an 8-inch square cookie pan.

Beat together with a wooden spoon until "liquidy" the sugar, eggs and vanilla. Mix in flour and salt. Add walnuts and mix well. At this point the batter will be thick and sticky and hard to mix.

Spread batter in pan. Start by pushing batter into corners with the wooden spoon and finish by patting into an even layer with your fingers and the palm of the hand.

Bake cookies 20 minutes, or until lightly brown and edges of the batter pull away from the sides of the pan.

Remove from oven and place pan on cooling rack for 10 minutes. While cookies are still warm, cut into large squares.

To frost, sprinkle carob chips on top as soon as cookies come out of the oven. The heat will soften the chips, and they can be spread with a butter knife and light touch.

Miscellaneous

Back at Kallimos . . .

At first, I was shy about chanting along with Haleigh in the garden. It seemed silly to think that chanting would help a garden. It seemed even sillier to think that one song should be sung while weeding but not while harvesting, and another should be sung while watering but only when the moon is in its waning phase.

When Haleigh told me that these rules exist because the songs are magic and must be used with great care, it was my turn to laugh. Now that I've seen with my own eyes her fantastic ability to cultivate the earth, I have become a believer. There may be no supporting research to back it up, but with results like hers, who cares?

Excerpted from Learning from Hannah © *William H. Thomas, M.D.*

ALMOND BUTTER

Makes 1 cup   *Roast at 300*

1-1/2 cups almonds   **1 tablespoon tahini, optional**

Preheat oven to 300 degrees.

Roast almonds on a cookie sheet in oven for 10-20 minutes. Watch carefully so they do not burn.

Place all but 1/4 cup of the almonds in the workbowl of a food processor fitted with the steel blade, or in a blender. Blend until smooth. Chop the reserved nuts into nut butter with several on/off turns of either machine.

Almonds can be also ground into nut butter without roasting first. If nut butter is not "liquidy" enough, add 1 tablespoon tahini.

Cashew butter: Roast cashews 10-15 minutes. Blend until the consistency desired. Chop in 1/4 cup of the nuts at the last minute for chunky-style nut butter.

Peanut butter: Roast peanuts for 20 minutes. Blend until the consistency desired. Also chop in 1/4 cup of the nuts at the last minute for chunky-style nut butter.

To make a sweet nut butter, blend in honey and a dash of cinnamon to taste.

APPLE CIDER SYRUP

Makes about 4 cups

To make cider syrup, fresh cider, juiced not more than 1/2 hour prior to boiling must be used, otherwise the necessary pectin will not be active.

Use cider syrup as you would maple syrup.

Enough apples to juice to make one gallon cider

Using a vegetable juicer, juice enough apples to make 1 gallon cider.

Boil cider at about 219 degrees until reduced to syrup. (Cider is acidic and should be boiled in stainless steel or enamel pots only.)

Boiling to the syrup stage will take several hours. To reduce boiling time, partially freeze cider. Use the sweet portion, which freezes last, for boiling.

When the cider is reduced to syrup, store in glass jars in the refrigerator.

DEBRA'S FAMOUS COLD REMEDY

Enough medicine to kill many colds

This remedy works! My son, Adam, says I used to torture him with it when he was too little to appreciate its effectiveness. My brother, Daniel, took it on a bike trip to Nova Scotia and said it saved his vacation. If your throat hurts too much to swallow, this will act like balm.

1 cup raw honey　　　　　　　**1-2 tablespoons prepared**
1-2 tablespoons cayenne pepper　　**horseradish**

Place honey in a glass jar. Add pepper and horseradish. Stir until liquidy.

Store cold remedy in the refrigerator until you feel something coming on or have a sore throat. When you use this remedy, take a 1/16 teaspoon dose or just a tiny dot. True, you will feel the heat and may think you are dying, but the honey will coat the throat, the red pepper will warm it and stop the hurt. We all know that horseradish opens blocked passages. Cayenne pepper is rich in vitamin C, higher even than orange juice.

Take remedy as needed.

So, stop laughing and mix some up today when you're feeling healthy. When you're sick, you won't feel like doing anything.

DEBRA'S OLIVE OIL VINAIGRETTE

Makes 6 cups

Worth making a large batch to keep in the refrigerator so that dressing will always be ready when you are!

4 cups olive oil	2 teaspoons salt
1 cup lemon juice	2 teaspoons black pepper
1 cup cider vinegar	1/2 teaspoon each basil,
10 cloves garlic, mashed	oregano, thyme
in garlic press	1 teaspoon mustard powder

Combine all dressing ingredients with a wire whisk in a bowl. Or whisk everything together in an 8-cup measuring cup, which saves having to wash extra measuring cups.

Keep dressing ready in jars in the refrigerator, where it may cloud up or become semi-solid because of the cold. Bring to room temperature and shake before using.

FRUIT SMOOTHIES

Makes 2 drinks

2 bananas
2 cups milk or soy milk
1 teaspoon vanilla
2 eggs, placed in boiling
  water for 30 seconds and
  removed

2 tablespoons honey or
  maple syrup
1/2 teaspoon brewers yeast

Using an electric blender, blend all ingredients until no pieces of banana remain. Chill drink 1 hour. Blend again for several seconds and serve in tall frosty glasses.

Frozen bananas may be used to eliminate chilling time. Freeze bananas when ripe. (Peel and place in the freezer on cookie sheets. Once frozen, remove from cookie sheets and store in plastic bags.

continued . . .

FRUIT SMOOTHIES
(continued)

Makes 2 drinks

2 ripe bananas
2/3 cup papaya juice

4 cups mixed fruit, some frozen

Using an electric blender, blend all ingredients until no pieces of banana remain. Serve in tall frosty glasses.

We like to freeze cut-up watermelon to make the smoothie very refreshing. Strawberries and blueberries give the drink a beautiful rosy color. Using mostly frozen fresh fruit results in a wonderful, thick smoothie, almost like ice cream. Use a rubber spatula to help the blender cope with all that frozen fruit.

GARLIC SAUCE

Makes about 3/4 cup

A nice simple sauce to use as a last-minute marinade.

4 cloves garlic
1/2 cup olive oil

1/4 cup lemon juice
salt and red pepper to taste

Using a food processor or blender, blend ingredients until smooth.

Use garlic sauce to brush chicken or fish before broiling or while grilling, or serve garlic sauce as a main course dip at the table.

Store in a glass jar in the refrigerator. Nice to have on hand to spice up an otherwise plain dish!

Try adding orange juice in place of lemon, 1/4 cup tomato juice, a teaspoon each paprika, cumin, oregano, pepper and the 4 cloves garlic to make a Mexican Sauce for Marinade.

GOMASIO

Makes 4-1/2 cups

Gomasio is a sesame flavored salt. Sesame seeds are an excellent source of protein and are rich in calcium.

1/2 cup sea salt   **4 cups whole brown sesame seeds**

Heat salt in a large skillet over a moderate flame. Set aside in a bowl.

Toast sesame seeds in the same skillet, stirring over medium-high heat for 5-10 minutes until slightly browned and aromatic. Seeds will begin to pop. Be careful not to burn!

Coarsely grind sesame seeds and salt using the steel blade of a food processor and on/off turns.

Store gomasio in airtight containers (Glass jars are good). A teaspoon of brown rice may be added to absorb any moisture and prevent clumping.

Use gomasio as you would salt - on salad, over cooked vegetables, grains, fish, or poultry.

HERB-INFUSED OIL

Fill a bottle half full of washed and dried fresh herb leaves. Fill bottle with olive oil. Cover tightly and steep for a week or two in a cool, dark place. Strain oil into another jar or bottle. Add several sprigs of herbs before covering and storing in the refrigerator.

Try combinations of herbs and some lemon wedges, too.

FRUIT-FLAVORED VINEGAR

In an enamel or stainless steel pan, bring 1 quart cider vinegar to a simmer. Add 2 cups berries and let mixture stand off the heat for 10 minutes. Pour vinegar and fruit into a jar and cover. Steep for 10-20 days and enjoy liberally. This is especially beautiful with raspberries. Try this with rose petals from unsprayed roses as well.

HERB-FLAVORED VINEGAR

Spread washed and dried fresh herb leaves on a cookie sheet. Dry away from sunlight until the leaves begin to curl. In a jar, place one cup packed herbs leaves together with one pint cider vinegar. Cover. Let jar stand for two weeks on a sunny window ledge. Shake jar once or twice each day. When the flavor is strong enough for your taste, strain into a clean jar, add herbs if desired and begin to use.

HORSERADISH

Makes a lot! (Depends on the root you choose.)

Be careful when making horseradish! Follow the directions below. If you like the red variety, add half a fresh beet. Horseradish prepared this way will keep for months in the refrigerator.

1 large horseradish root　　　　　**2 teaspoons salt**
1-1/4 cups cider vinegar

Scrub horseradish root with a stiff-bristled brush to remove dirt. Peel it and cut into 1-inch pieces.

Using the steel blade of a food processor and on/off turns, chop horseradish. With the machine running, add vinegar and salt. Process until horseradish is smooth.

Do not open workbowl for 5 minutes to give the fumes a chance to settle. If the root is a powerful one and the lid is removed too soon, your eyes will tear and your throat will burn. Be careful!

Spoon horseradish into glass jars and store in the refrigerator. Horseradish may "burn" the inside of metal jar covers and the top of the horseradish may brown over time as it dries out, but the underneath layers will still be fine and potent enough to use.

Use horseradish in Debra's Famous Cold Remedy, as well as to accompany fish or chicken.

MAYONNAISE

Makes 1 cup

1 egg
1/2 teaspoon salt
1/2 teaspoon dry mustard
1 tablespoon cider vinegar

1 tablespoon lemon juice
1 cup oil (olive, almond, walnut,
   or safflower), at room
   temperature

Using the steel blade of a food processor, blend egg, salt, mustard, vinegar, lemon juice and a few drops of oil.

With the machine running, slowly pour remaining oil through the feed tube in a steady stream. That's all there is to it!

Store mayonnaise in a glass jar in the refrigerator until ready to use.

For a thicker mayonnaise, add 1/4 cup more oil.

Other options: Leave out mustard; try adding a teaspoon of honey or more to taste. Use safflower oil when making a sweetened or milder mayonnaise.

To make "green" mayonnaise, chop 1-1/2 cups combined and loosely packed watercress, tarragon, chives, or parsley with the food processor. Strain mixture through a fine-meshed strainer or cheesecloth. Mix juice into mayonnaise. (Reserve greens for use in soup or stews.)

MUSTARD MARINADE

Makes about 1 cup marinade

1 onion, quartered	**4 tablespoons lemon juice**
1 teaspoon dried parsley	**1 tablespoon thyme**
2 tablespoons Dijon mustard	**1 teaspoon tarragon**

Using the steel blade of a food processor, or a blender, blend ingredients. Use to pour over chicken, fish or tofu and marinate for at least 30 minutes. Broil chicken, fish or tofu in marinade.

GINGER MARINADE

Makes about 1 cup marinade

1 onion, quartered	**2 tablespoons tamari soy sauce**
2 cloves garlic	**1 teaspoon lemon juice**
1 teaspoon ginger	

Using the steel blade of a food processor, or a blender, blend marinade. Use to pour over chicken, fish or tofu and marinate for at least 30 minutes. Broil chicken, fish or tofu in marinade.

OLD-FASHIONED DILL PICKLES

Makes lots of pickles

Cut cucumbers into 2-inch chunks, or leave whole. Grape leaves are used as a natural preservative and to keep pickles firm.

1-1/2 quarts cider vinegar	1 cup fresh dill weed
4 quarts water	12 cloves peeled garlic
fresh grape leaves	3 bay leaves
6 pounds pickling cucumbers	2 tablespoons black
1-1/2 cups salt	peppercorns

Combine water and vinegar.

Place some grape leaves on the bottom of glass jars or a large ceramic crock. Pack container(s) with cucumbers. Fill with vinegar and water, adding more water if necessary for container to be full. Pour liquid off cucumbers (Now you have the exact amount) into the pan. Bring liquid to a boil. Add salt and stir until dissolved.

Add dill, garlic, bay leaves, and peppercorns to cucumbers. Cover with more grape leaves. Pour brine over cucumbers so that pickles and leaves are completely covered. Use a heavy, clean stone or dish to keep cucumbers submerged if not wedged tightly under liquid.

Set jars or crock aside, covered, for 2 days. After 2 days, refrigerate pickles. They are ready to start eating when half-sour, after a day.

Reuse brine to pickle Jerusalem artichokes or other vegetables.

RAW CRANBERRY RELISH

Makes about 10 cups

A nice change from cooked and sugared cranberry sauce. Cranberry relish keeps for two weeks in the refrigerator and also freezes well.

4 cups raw cranberries
3 medium oranges, quartered,
   seeded and peeled
3 large apples, quartered, cored
   and peeled

1 cup honey or fruit juice
   concentrate
1/2 teaspoon cinnamon

Using the steel blade of a food processor, coarsely chop cranberries, oranges, and apples with on/off turns. Stop the machine once or twice to scrape down the sides of the workbowl with a rubber spatula.

Put the chopped fruit in a large bowl. Add honey and cinnamon and mix well. Refrigerate cranberry relish in glass jars.

In addition to serving cranberry relish with poultry, try mixing with unflavored yogurt for a quick snack.

STRAWBERRY ORANGE COOLER

Makes 2 drinks

1 pint frozen strawberries	**2 tablespoons honey or**
1 cup orange juice	**more to taste**
1 cup yogurt	**1/2 teaspoon brewers yeast**

Using an electric blender, blend all ingredients until the berries move smoothly under the blade.

Serve at once in tall frosty glasses.

Strawberries can be purchased frozen, or frozen when they are plentiful in the summer. Wash, hull and place on cookie sheets in the freezer. Once frozen, remove and store in air-tight containers or plastic bags.

NUT MILKS

Makes about 5 cups

1 cup nuts, almond	**3-4 cups water**
cashew, peanut, or	**4 pitted dates**
sunflower	

Using an electric blender, liquefy nuts and water until a milky consistency. Adding the dates makes the milk sweeter and thicker.

SUMMER PESTO

Makes about 3 cups

Serve pesto with fettuccine, use in calzones, or stir a spoonful into stews or soups. Use to season fish or poultry.

Store pesto in small glass jars in the refrigerator for several days, or make pesto "ice cubes" and store in plastic baggies in the freezer.

2 cups packed parsley	**1/2 teaspoon black pepper**
1 large bunch fresh basil	**1/4 teaspoon cayenne pepper**
1/2 cup olive oil	**1/2 teaspoon oregano**
4 cloves garlic	**1/2 cup pine nuts or walnuts**
1/2 cup grated Pecorino Romano	

Using the steel blade of a food processor, blend ingredients until smooth, stopping the machine as needed to scrape down the sides of the workbowl with a rubber spatula.

Pesto is wonderful. Always have some on hand to dress up a plain dish. Make in the summer when fresh basil is plentiful.

WINTER PESTO

Makes about 4-1/2 cups

Winter pesto reminds one of summer. So let it snow and have the best of both seasons!

12 ounces fresh spinach
1 bunch parsley
1/3 cup lemon juice
1 cup olive oil
2/3 cup pine nuts or almonds or walnuts

1 cup grated Pecorino Romano
1/3 cup dried basil
6 cloves garlic
1/4 teaspooon cayenne
1 teaspoon black pepper

Wash the spinach and parsley and spin-dry in a salad spinner.

Using the steel blade of a food processor, blend half the spinach and parsley with the remaining ingredients. When the mixture is smooth, add remaining greens. Process until pesto is a paste.

Use winter pesto just as you would summer pesto.

ZAATAR

Makes about 2-1/4 cups

This comes from Lebanon. Use over salad, rice, beans, fish, chicken. Zaatar is said to aid digestion and to clear up skin problems!

**4 tablespoons brown sesame
  seeds
1 cup oregano**

**1 cup ground sumac
2 tablespoons salt**

In a skillet, dry-roast sesame seeds over low heat until they become fragrant and begin to pop. Add oregano, sumac and salt and stir 1 minute. Remove from heat.

Cool and store zaatar in glass jars. Use as you would salt.

Message from the Author

I was fortunate to have been brought up on natural foods before they became popular and before people began worrying that processed and refined foods might be making them sick. As a child, my mother used to make us fresh vegetable juice to drink when we got home from school. She also ordered organic grains from California, which she would grind to make her own flour for bread. On a business trip to Hawaii, my father brought home a case of pineapples. In a typically Stark manner, those tops were planted in the front yard around a huge oak tree and, in time, supplied us and some of the neighborhood with fresh pineapples in an era when most people believed pineapples grew in cans.

As a child, I watched my grandmother swirl eggs in a blue-and-white speckled enamel fry pan to make blintz shells without flour. From another grandmother, I learned what compote was. I learned to pickle a duck with garlic and to enhance a peach or cherry dish with almond. To this day, getting together in our family means getting together to share food and conversation.

When I was in my teens, the family orthodontist offered to tear up his bill and pay my mother fifty dollars per loaf for two loaves of her homemade seed bread. At this, my interest in food took a serious turn.

People say they'd like to eat natural foods but can't afford them. However, if one compares nutrients, unit for unit, and if one takes into account the greater health and well-being that real foods bring us (especially as we get older and our bodies start to wear down), the reduced number of visits to doctors and dentists, and the sheer pleasure one gets from eating good food, I believe that in the long run, natural foods turn out to be the better buy.

Acknowledgments

My love to my parents, Beatrice and Sidney Stark, and to my brothers, David and Daniel Stark, with whom I share memories of conversations around the dining table and without whom there would be no Debra's Natural Gourmet food store. To my son, Adam, who helped eat the bloopers during the two years it took to compile the recipes in this book. To Mary Kadlik who tested each recipe and gave her honest and loving feedback, and to my husband, Yossi, who eats whatever I give him and who makes the best omelettes ever.

Index

Did you enjoy visiting Kallimos?

You're not alone if you found yourself wishing
the excerpts about Kallimos were longer. Here's what
others have said about *Learning from Hannah:
Secrets for a Life Worth Living*.

"*Learning from Hannah* is a testament to the human spirit, wherein
author William Thomas reveals a gift for storytelling and for conjuring
up a wonderful world where the wisdom of the elders has built a life
worth living for all. A splendidly visionary novel and wonderfully
inspired reading."—Midwest Book Review

"Like a fable, *Learning from Hannah* divulges deep truths about human
nature while imparting a timeless moral message."—The Small Press
Book Review

"This is a life-affirming, multi-layered book . . . a delightful way to learn
about going ahead with life in a positive fashion."—Crone Chronicles

Independent Press Award
Finalist in Visionary Fiction

Go ahead. Buy the book. You'll be glad you did!
Money-back guarantee if you're not delighted
with your purchase.

1-800-789-7916
www.vandb.com

Also available at bricks-and-mortar and online bookstores everywhere.

Or send a check for $21.95 plus $4.95 s/h to
VanderWyk & Burnham, PO Box 2789-K, Acton, MA 01720.